Understanding Marxism

A CANADIAN INTRODUCTION

FRANK CUNNINGHAM

Understanding Marxism

A CANADIAN INTRODUCTION

FRANK CUNNINGHAM

PROGRESS BOOKS TORONTO 1981

First Printing 1978
Second Printing 1981

ISBN 0-919396-42-9

Cover and book design: Brian Harrod

Printing: Eveready Printers, Toronto

Published by Progress Books
71 Bathurst Street
Toronto, Ontario, Canada M5V 2P6

Canadian Cataloguing in Publication Data

Cunningham, Frank, 1940-
  Understanding Marxism

Includes index.
ISBN 0-919396-42-9 pa.

1. Socialism. 2. Socialism in Canada.
I. Title

HX36.C85   335.4   C78-001147-3

Contents

ACKNOWLEDGMENTS

Thanks are due to the following
people who read drafts of this book and
made valuable criticisms and suggestions to
improve it: Barbara Cameron, Nelson Clarke,
Phyllis Clarke, Enza DiTrani, Robin Endres,
Dan Goldstick, Charnie Guettel, Robert Kenny,
Kelly Pykerman, Maryka Omatsu, William
Sydney, Lesley Towers, Ken Van Male.
Thanks also to Maggie Bizzell and the staff
of Progress Books for help in final
preparation of the manuscript.

Chapter 1

SCIENTIFIC SOCIALISM

Try the following experiment with your friends, co-workers or classmates. First ask them what they think Marxism means. Everyone will have something to say, such as one of the following wrong answers:

> "It's the theory of communism; therefore it's against democracy."
>
> "It thinks everyone should be the same."
>
> "It reduces everything to economics."
>
> "It's the unrealistic belief in a cooperative society."
>
> "It's a subversive theory that preaches violence and terror through revolution."

Now ask your friends how they know this. Have they read anything by Marx, Engels or Lenin, or have they heard Marxism explained by someone who actually agrees with it? In most cases the people you question haven't read anything by a Marxist; nor have they discussed Marxism with anyone who both agrees with the theory and can explain it. The exceptions are probably those who have read sections of something like the *Communist Manifesto* in a high-school social studies course, but because of the boring way the course was taught they remember little about what they read.

Why is it that although most Canadians have not been exposed to a sympathetic explanation of Marxism, all have views on the subject, and sometimes very strong views? The answer, of course, is that we all learn how bad Marxism is supposed to be — or how it doesn't work — in school, in the newspapers and magazines and on T.V.

But why is this? In my job as a teacher of social and political philosophy I encounter dozens of theories about history and society. New ones, or variations of old ones, are invented every few years. Why don't the major sources of "information" and "education" in our country tell us how to think about these new theories as well?

Again, the answer is not hard to find. Marxism is not just one theory among others. Its founders called it "scientific socialism" because it is a scientific theory intended to help working people change a society of private ownership into a socialist society. Marxism already *has* helped about a third of the world's population to succeed in this task.

In large parts of the industrialized world and among many less developed countries close to socialism, Marxism is the leading perspective. The reason we are told what to think about Marxism is because it is an actual world force that is *feared* by those, like the owners of big monopolies, who stand to lose something (their super-profits) whenever working people succeed in gaining socialism.

Canadian working people need Marxism to understand the sources of the problems that confront us, such as unemployment, rising prices and the lack of control over how we live and work. We need Marxism to help us take control of our own lives and change society into one that answers our needs. What working people need in this country are not myths and distorted versions of Marxism, that is, what anti-socialists want us to believe about it, but an understanding of the actual principles of scientific socialism.

This book is meant to help Canadian working people gain this understanding by introducing the most important views of Marxism and defending them against their most common criticisms.

MARXISM

Marxism grew out of the political and economic struggles of nineteenth-century Europe. It developed from previous work done by economists and philosophers going back yet a century earlier and from the efforts of working people to organize themselves against capitalism. Karl Marx and Frederick Engels put their skills at the disposal of these revolutionary workers. They brought together previous thought and advanced it to serve working-class needs, developing the theory wherever the police would let them, mainly in Germany, France and England.

In the appendix to this book, I have included a short sketch of the lives of Marx and Engels and also of V.I. Lenin, who further

2

advanced Marxism, and references will be made to their works at the end of each chapter.

Marxism concludes that war, inequality, and poverty cannot finally be eliminated from the world until large-scale private ownership of the means of production is eliminated. Naturally enough, big businessmen have not appreciated the theory much. From the beginning they have tried to suppress or discredit Marxism, a task that has been made easier for them since they have a large say in what is taught in the schools, what books are printed, and what is said in newspapers and on radio and television. During the cold war in the 1950s Marxism was rather effectively suppressed in North America. Only a few books by Marxists were available, and these could only be found in certain book stores. Marxists were barred from teaching, film-making, publishing, and so on. People's growing frustrations about their problems and democratic resistance to cold-war policies finally changed the political climate, although it is still harder to find out what Marx said about capitalism than it is to find out what some astrologer or other crank says about anything at all.

Now, as before, there are a variety of ways used to discredit Marxism. One method is to confuse people about its scientific nature. Since it was Engels and Lenin who *explicitly* argued in favour of the need for a scientific approach to society, some "scholars" of Marx have attempted to separate Marx's ideas from those of Engels and Lenin. In this book I will be writing about the theory common to Marx and Engels and developed by Lenin and other Marxists. Readers who are worried about this approach will find my justifications in the appendix.

Another, more common, attempt to discredit Marxism has been to classify it as a kind of religion that Marxists dogmatically hold as a matter of faith. Although there are some who like to think of themselves as Marxists and who do regard it in this way, nothing could be further from the truth. Marxism is the theory Marx and Engels developed from practical experience and much painstaking scientific research. They, and others since them, have continued to follow the theory because further research has confirmed its basic insights, and it has actually worked in practice.

Perhaps its growth provides the best example of the scientific nature of Marxism. In spite of anti-Marxist claims it is completely against the basic principles of Marxism to relate everything back to a few sacred texts that are supposed to be the last word. In the light of advancing experience and knowledge, Marxism has been added to and improved over the past hundred years.

Lenin was instrumental in expanding the theory to take imperialism into account, and other Marxists throughout the world have been busy applying, testing and developing the theory in practically every field of inquiry — economics, history, culture and natural science.

Another attempt to discredit Marxism in Canada has been to label it as something that does not apply to Canadian conditions. I will discuss this allegation in the last chapter, and in the course of the book I will indicate some of the ways I think Marxism applies to us. The allegation is sometimes based on the fact that socialism does not appear to be just around the corner here. Despite Marx's and Engels' optimistic calculations about how soon some socialist revolutions would occur, Marxism does not lead one to expect that revolutions in countries like Canada are easily won. In any case, before judging whether Marxism can be applied some place it is necessary to understand what the theory actually *is* rather than what some anti-Marxist claims it is.

Sometimes it is said that Marxism does not apply to Canada because Canadian working people are not interested in socialism; hence theories designed to help them conduct effective compaigns for socialism are useless. Despite attempts of the pro-capitalist media to portray Canadians as complacent supporters of capitalism, some Canadian working people are far from satisfied with the *status quo* and want a socialist Canada. Many more, also dissatisfied, are at least open to the idea.

SOCIALISM

A socialist society is one in which the major means of production and distribution (factories, mines, large food and clothing chains, and so on), as well as financial institutions like the banks are owned and controlled by the working people of that society. Marxist theoreticians did not invent this concept, and they did not discover that it is in the best interests of working people to gain socialism. The idea grew out of working people's movements themselves. What Marxists have provided is a scientific theory of human society, human history and the relation of humans to their natural environment. Without a scientific understanding of these things it would be impossible for working people to take control of society and govern it in their own interests. Marxism is called "scientific socialism" for this very reason. Its scientific nature also explains why it has been no accident that successful socialist movements have been guided by Marxism.

While Marxists did not invent the idea of socialism, they have refined it in very important and practical ways. This is especially true of the Marxist concepts of "revolution" and of the "state." When anti-socialists today talk about revolution, they conjure up images of irrational violence in which masses of people, ruthlessly led by self-seeking manipulators, run amuck. Mind you, when these same anti-socialists are from countries like France or the United States where capitalist forms of society were themselves secured by violent revolution (the French Revolution of 1789 and the American Revolution of 1776), they refer to *these* revolutions almost in a religious way as the best things that have ever happened in human history. Marxism replaces both these biased ideas of revolution with a concept that is scientifically useful for understanding the actual nature of important historical changes.

In the Marxist view a social revolution is the basic and thoroughgoing transformation of a society that takes place when one social and economic class succeeds in taking political power away from another class and uses this power to reorganize society to serve its own interests. For instance, in the French Revolution of 1789, merchants and manufacturers, aided by other classes and groups, took power from the feudal king and reorganized society to promote the acquisition of profit through trade and industry. This revolution was accompanied by violent armed combat, as were later *socialist* revolutions like the Russian Revolution of 1917. This is not because the classes that want revolution also happen to like bloodshed, but because in a social revolution the classes that lose power are prepared to turn to arms, even if they have lost their power through completely democratic procedures.

A careful study of any social revolution bears out the fact that where there has been violence, this has not been because revolutionaries wanted it, but because they were driven to it in self-defence. For the Marxist the only sense in which all social revolutions must necessarily be "violent" is that they involve basic and far-reaching changes in the whole of a society.

When Marxists say that revolutions involve a class taking political power, they are referring to the power of the state. Marxists recognize that the state (the government, the army and police, courts of law, a professional civil service and so on) is not a neutral body that somehow exists outside the efforts of working people to make a better life for themselves.

Under the capitalist system of private ownership of the means of production and distribution, the state actually combats the efforts of working people and serves the interests of big business instead. Under socialism the state is an instrument used by working people to guide and protect their society. With this view of the state Marxists have been able to distinguish socialism from "social democracy" or the "welfare state" on the one hand and from the stateless society of "communism" on the other.

Unlike Cuba, for example, Canada is not a socialist country. Neither are "social-democratic" countries, where the government in some ways plays a larger role in regulating the economy. Current examples are England and the Federal Republic of Germany ("West Germany"). It is true that some important social services have been gained by working people in some of these countries, as, for example, in Sweden, when it had a social-democratic government. However, the most profitable large means of production and distribution are still owned by private business, and governments in these social-democratic countries regulate their economies to maintain the profits of the largest corporations, but not to eliminate inflation or unemployment. Most importantly, these states do not build a society geared to people's needs. Instead, as in Canada, each gain for working people must be fought for by them, and there is the constant threat that existing gains will be taken away. Failure to distinguish between socialism and these forms of "regulated capitalism" keeps working people from seeing that they must take control of the state and reorganize it to serve their own interests.

"Communism" is sometimes used to refer to the theories and efforts of Communist Parties. Marxists use "communism" also to refer to a stage of human society, which will *follow* the successful building of socialism. In communist societies, as under socialism, the means of production and distribution will be socially owned and controlled, but unlike previous societies, including socialist ones, the massive apparatus of the army, a professional administration, and other parts of the state will no longer be needed. While socialism lays the basis for communism, there are no communist societies in this technical Marxist sense of the word yet, and until capitalism has been virtually eliminated from the globe, such a society is probably impossible.

Failure to distinguish between socialism and communism leads to a misunderstanding of socialist revolutions and of the efforts to build socialism. A socialist revolution occurs when the working class takes state power and dismantles those aspects of the state

6

that serve the interests of private ownership. The working people rebuild the state to serve themselves.

Creating a working people's state is of crucial importance. First of all it is no small task to reconstruct a society that has been geared to the private profit of large corporations. The educational systems, communications and entertainment facilities, cultural institutions, public services of all sorts, not to mention the economy itself, all need to be transformed to serve working people, and a state apparatus is needed for this.

In the second place, no movement for socialism and no attempt to preserve and build socialism has been free from anti-socialist attempts at economic and military sabotage. Such attempts failed to prevent socialism in Russia, China, Cuba and Vietnam, but succeeded in setting socialism back in other places, such as in the 1973 U.S.-inspired fascist coup in Chile. While transitions from socialism to communism will be peaceful, socialist revolutions are always accompanied by the threat of violence — through no fault of the pro-socialist forces. A *peaceful* socialist revolution, such as one achieved through elections, is obviously something to be hoped and worked for (only a lunatic would think otherwise). But it must be recognized that capitalist forces will always turn to violence if they can get away with it. A peaceful socialist revolution would require such overwhelmingly strong support that anti-socialists couldn't even attempt violence against it.

Marxists know that a pro-capitalist state will not give socialist revolution to working people. Nor can it be willed into existence or achieved without danger and struggle. To win and build socialism against the wishes of powerful enemies it is necessary to create the broadest possible support. Just how difficult this is has been shown more than once by the problems and mistakes of socialist movements and governments. The task requires an understanding of the balance of forces in a country and in the world, of the level of people's political consciousness, of the nature of people's struggles, and of a vast number of other economic and political realities. For all this a correct scientific theory of society is needed, and Marxism is that theory.

READINGS FOR CHAPTER ONE

At the end of each chapter, I will list some of the classic works by Marx, Engels, Lenin, and will occasionally note books by Marxists that relate to the subject matter of the chapter. I have not attempted to list all of the books and articles, classic and more recent, pro-Marxist and anti-Marxist, that someone who wanted to become an expert on Marxism would have to read.

I will refer to primary sources by their titles only. They can be found individually or in collections of Marx, Engels and Lenin's writings. The complete set of Lenin's works is available in English in 45 volumes: *V.I. Lenin, Collected Works,* (Moscow, 1966). The complete English translation of the works of Marx and Engels is right now in the process of being published. It will run to 50 volumes, and, like Lenin's *Collected Works,* will be available in most large libraries and in progressive book stores.

Some relatively inexpensive books containing important writings of Marx, Engels, and Lenin are:

Karl Marx and Frederick Engels, Selected Works (Moscow and New York, 1968). The New York edition (reprinted in 1977) is in International Publishers' New World Paperback series.

V.I. Lenin, Selected Works (Moscow, 1968, reprinted, 1975).

Two other books, both in New World Paperbacks, that are worth acquiring are:

Reader in Marxist Philosophy, edited by H. Selsam and H. Martel (New York, 1963, reprinted 1977).

Dynamics of Social Change, edited by H. Selsam, D. Goldway, and H. Martel (New York, 1970, reprinted 1975).

These two books contain selections, grouped by topic, from different books, pamphlets, and letters of Marx, Engels, and Lenin.

Good introductions to Marxism by its founders are:

V.I. Lenin, *The Three Sources and Three Components Parts of Marxism.*

K. Marx & F. Engels, *The Manifesto of the Communist Party.*

F. Engels, *Socialism, Utopian and Scientific.*

Chapter 2

WORKING-CLASS RULE AND HUMAN NATURE

Under capitalism the major means of production and distribution are privately owned by a small handful of people whose property and the profits they extract from it are protected by a pro-capitalist state. Capitalist economy is based on *competition*. In socialism the major means of production and distribution are publicly owned and the society is governed by a working-class state. The economy is based on cooperation. Decisions about what to produce, how much to produce, what wages and prices should be, and so on, are based on estimates of what is best for the entire society rather than for the profits of individual, capitalist owners.

Socialism is the worst possible nightmare of capitalists since it runs counter to everything they believe and, more importantly, since it challenges their profits. Therefore, it is not surprising that they promote the opinion that a cooperative society governed by the working class is against human nature. Pro-capitalists have advanced many arguments to show either that a socialist society is impossible or that it is undesirable. The main arguments that socialism is against human nature are: (1) that it would dampen individual incentive; (2) that it would hold back the best people so that the "fittest" would not survive; (3) that it is unfair to people who are naturally better than other people; and (4) that a cooperative society is impossible since people are naturally selfish.

Put together, these four arguments form the capitalist view that societies must always be ruled by a selfish elite who deserve to rule because they are "naturally" better than others. In one way or another, the attitudes expressed by the arguments are found in the movies and on T.V., in popular literature, and in the schools. Unfortunately, a capitalist, competitive society like ours creates things like selfishness and inequality, so to some extent the arguments match people's experience. It is worthwhile to examine each of these arguments against socialism.

The argument about incentives starts from the fact, which Marxists and everybody else recognize, that people will not work indefinitely or strive to improve themselves unless they think something is to be gained by it, if not for their own generation, then at least for their children's. But the anti-socialist wants to conclude from this that in a cooperative society people will not have the incentive to work and improve themselves. Why not? As Marxists maintain and contemporary history is already proving, cooperative societies are more efficient at providing a decent standard of living for the entire population; so wouldn't people have *more* incentive in a socialist society than in a capitalist one? Very few people still believe the capitalist myth that anybody can become rich. Many people are born into economic poverty or into systems of racial or ethnic discrimination from which they know there is little likelihood of escape under the present system.

Sometimes advocates of the incentive argument try to turn the example of present-day socialist societies into evidence for their own case. They claim that these societies have had to adopt competitive measures in the form of economic incentives. While the income differences under socialism are quite narrow compared to those under capitalism, skilled jobs still pay higher than less skilled ones, and there are economic incentives to reward high production within some industries. Actually, socialism, unlike capitalism, frequently pays more to people who do particularly unpleasant jobs.

Economic incentives in socialism, far from contradicting economic cooperation, are part and parcel of it. Training people in certain skills and increasing production in a certain industry are cooperative decisions in socialist society and are for the good of society as a whole. One way of accomplishing this is to pay people more for acquiring those skills or for stepping up production.

The argument about incentives supposes a false view of the nature of socialist societies. Socialism does not immediately eliminate all economic problems, and it does not magically create people who are willing and able to make large sacrifices with no hope of personally gaining from their work. The pro-capitalist often paints a completely unrealistic picture of what "true socialism" should be and then argues that socialism has failed because it does not match this idea.

All this serves to blur the fact that "true socialism" is not an imaginary idea, but an actual form of social organization. Depending on the particular conditions, socialist societies take a variety of measures in the interests of the working class. They build industries; they increase production here, decrease it there; they find ways to market goods; they centralize some parts of the economy, decentralize others; and, within limits, they encourage the development of certain skills or increased production by the use of incentives. To the extent that these and other measures do in fact serve working people's interests by creating a better life for them and their children, the system of socialist cooperation succeeds.

SURVIVAL OF THE FITTEST

The argument that in a cooperative society the weak would drag down the strong is a version of a theory called "Social Darwinism." Charles Darwin, the great nineteenth-century biologist for whom Marx and Engels had the highest respect, developed a theory of evolution in the animal world, called by some the "survival of the fittest" theory. Darwin showed how species of animals survived to the extent that they were well equipped to obtain food and shelter in their environment. Species that could not adapt to changes in their environment were not well equipped and died off. *Social* Darwinists are pro-capitalist social scientists who claim to apply Darwin's theory *within* human societies. They maintain that in a competitive system, those who are well equipped to survive, that is, those who are smart, strong and imaginative, rise to the "top" (become capitalists), and those who are not well equipped sink to the "bottom" (become workers) or even die off. In a cooperative society, these Social Darwinists maintain, the ill-equipped would overwhelm the strong and the human species would grow weaker and weaker.

By way of criticizing this view it is worth noting in the first place that almost all of those who are at the "top" in capitalist societies were born there. They did not get where they are by any characteristic other than having rich parents. This is more than just an oversight on the part of Social Darwinists. It reflects an entirely mistaken conception of human nature. It supposes that individual

11

people somehow come into the world with ready-made desires (for instance, to make super-profits) and with ready-made, individual abilities (for instance, to be a factory manager) and that society is a sort of arena where people try to satisfy their desires by using these abilities. This view ignores the fact that humans are *social* beings. What a person wants and what a person can do depend on the society that person lives in. It is thanks to the labour of millions of people stretching back through the centuries that there exists a system of factory production today so that somebody is able to become a factory manager. It is because there is an economic system of competition among individual owners that anybody can want to accumulate private super-profits. The Social Darwinists assume that individuals, or at least the individuals whom they consider worthy, are what they are independently of history and society.

Another problem with the Social Darwinist argument in favour of capitalism is that it misses the whole point of Darwin's own doctrine. Darwin was thinking about characteristics of entire species that make them likely to survive. Do the characteristics of capitalist competitiveness really contribute to the survival of the human species? Capitalism has dominated the world for less than 200 years, a very short period of time considering that the human species is about three million years old. But in that short period there have never been more than a few years at a time without a major war. Within months of its invention, the atom bomb was used twice by a capitalist government against civilians. Biochemical warfare has been "perfected." The atmosphere, land and water supplies of large parts of the planet have been polluted, and there have been regular cycles of economic inflation and depression.

Can anyone seriously hold that the capitalist system is conducive to the survival of our species? We'll be lucky to get rid of capitalism before it kills everybody. On the other hand, there are several reasons to suppose that a cooperative society run by the working class is conducive to survival. Everybody agrees that there is strength and safety in cooperation. Even the capitalists recognize this and are prepared to cooperate with one another when threatened by socialist revolution. A system based on cooperation should be a stronger and safer one for humans.

Unlike capitalists, the working class forms the majority of a society's population, and therefore workers have a stake in building a society that will serve the interests of most of the human species. In a socialist economy there are no such people as war profiteers so the risk of war is lessened. Finally, in present-day socialist countries, despite adverse conditions, cooperative economies have already eliminated such things as starvation and have created truly impressive systems of public health. All these things surely contribute to human survival, not the opposite.

The argument that socialism is unfair rests on the view that there are natural inequalities among people. It assumes that some people are naturally better and hence deserve more than other people. There are several things wrong with this argument. In the first place it is not very wise of capitalists to advance the argument, since most of them owe their privileged place in society to the accident of being born into rich families. Moreover, what are their special talents that make them so deserving? The ability to write checks? The ability to scheme and plot against one another and the people in order to make profits?

In the second place, nobody can deny that there are differences among people, that they have different skills and are better or worse at the same skills. The question to ask is whether capitalism or socialism allows people best to develop their skills, and which kind of society rewards people whose skills are really beneficial to the people of that society. The Marxist maintains that it is socialism that encourages and rewards worthwhile skills.

Another problem with this pro-capitalist argument is that it assumes the inequalities people have are inborn. However, a better case can be made that the skills people have in the main are acquired as they grow up. In Canada, as elsewhere in the capitalist world, education involves "streaming" where children from working-class and rural backgrounds are sent to schools that equip them only for certain kinds of work. Moreover, the quality of education is quite a bit lower in working-class schools than in middle- and upper-class schools. Classes are often more crowded; there are fewer facilities; and students are not encouraged to have a high opinion of their potentials. Surely these are important in determining how people develop their individual skills. Similarly, where there are differences of ability in people from the same economic backgrounds, these differences are more likely to be caused by factors in their environment than by some inborn ability.

The theory that there are inborn inequalities not only serves as a criticism of socialism. It is also used to justify the inequalities that

13

exist in capitalist society. I mentioned the differences in quality of education in capitalist countries. The following is a defence of these inequalities by the 1975 curriculum director of the Toronto Board of Education in response to the charge that the board does not give everybody a high level of education:

> Well, no, we're not, because everybody isn't capable of that — ability and intelligence just aren't equal. No society ever has had a majority of really literate people. (quoted in *Maclean's*, Sept., 1975, p. 3.)

Is it supposed to be an accident that all the "capable" students in Toronto are in the upper-class parts of the city?

SELFISHNESS

People are selfish to the extent that they are not prepared to make sacrifices for other people. A very widespread theory in capitalist society is that everybody is naturally selfish. This theory, like the others, is designed to protect capitalist interests against socialism. Socialism cannot be gained or constructed unless people unite with one another and are willing to cooperate. The task of gaining socialism is very difficult and requires the forging of alliances among the large majority of a society's population. It requires much long and difficult work on the part of many people. But, the argument goes, since people are selfish they will not trust one another enough to make alliances and they will not work for something unless they know they will personally gain from it.

In one sense this argument represents the daydreams of pro-capitalists and is irrelevant to whether or not people will struggle to build socialism. People strive for socialism when they find capitalism intolerable, when their needs and values and the possibilities of modern society cause them to see socialism as in their interests and capitalism as against their interests. In these circumstances, people will take the risks involved in socialist revolution or make the sacrifices necessary to gain and build socialism because they do not see any acceptable alternative.

The argument also presents a distorted view of human nature. It is certainly true that people are partially selfish, and it is no wonder. In a society based on competition and dominated by a class with no concern for the well-being of working people, people have to learn to look out for themselves. But at the same time, most people are also unselfish. In disasters like floods or fires a small minority take to looting. But most people will help complete strangers, often

14

making personal sacrifices or even risking their lives to do so. If everyone is entirely selfish by nature, then how can there be people who do not act selfishly?

If examples of non-selfish behaviour were very rare, then those exhibiting this behaviour could be explained away as abnormal. But unselfish behaviour is not rare. One does not need to look to fires and floods to find it. Many in our society, such as very old people and children, are relatively helpless, and some take advantage of this by cheating or robbing them. But most people do not. If everybody is completely selfish, then why not? Why don't people prey on anybody who is weaker than they whenever there is personal advantage to be gained with little risk? (An explanation sometimes given for the existence of people who make sacrifices for others is that they are really selfish after all, since they take pleasure in helping others. Well if this is to count as selfishness, then let there be more such "selfish"people!)

Recognizing that humans are capable of both selfish and of unselfish behaviour raises the question of *why* people sometimes act selfishly and sometimes unselfishly. There is no mystery. It depends on a person's social and economic circumstances. In a dog-eat-dog society such as is promoted by capitalism, where it is often impossible to get ahead except at someone else's expense and cooperativeness is often pictured as a sign of weakness, it is no surprise that many people often act selfishly.

Aggression. There are two common variations in the selfishness theory. One is that people are not only selfish but also hostile to other people or naturally aggressive. This view was expressed by the popular psychological theorist, Sigmund Freud:

> I cannot enquire into whether the abolition of private property is expedient or advantageous. But I am able to recognize that the psychological premises on which the system is based are an untenable illusion. In abolishing private property we deprive the human love of aggression of one of its instruments, certainly a strong one though certainly not the strongest; but we have in no way altered the differences in power and influence which are misused by aggressiveness, nor have we altered anything in its nature.

Freud was explicitly saying that socialism will not change human relations, since people are naturally aggressive and will

15

express their aggression some way or other. The clear message is, don't waste your time trying to change things.

This addition to the selfishness theory makes the theory less plausible. While there are people who are aggressive, they are the exception and not the rule. People who are regularly aggressive or hostile are usually spotted by those around them and thought of as having something wrong with them, not as being typical examples of humanity.

Private property. Another version of the selfishness theory is that everybody has a natural desire for private property. Some writers say that humans, like all other animals, have a "territorial imperative," which takes the form of striving for private property. This argument confuses private property with personal possessions. Of course people want to have some things they do not share. If everybody shared the same toothbrush, it would be impossible to brush in the morning due to the long queues, not to mention the danger of transmitting diseases. Also, there are only so many people who can share the same house or car. For that matter, only so many people can farm the same land or hunt in the same forest, which is why in tribal hunting and farming societies the land for each tribe was staked out. It makes sense for people to want personal access to certain things they need that cannot realistically be shared or can only be shared with a few.

On the other hand, the desire for "private property" is the desire to personally control things that people other than yourself need and could realistically share. Thus a man who privately owns a factory or a supermarket controls something that provides for the satisfaction of more than just his own needs or controls goods that can be realistically shared, as in socialist collective ownership. Even under capitalism, people attempt to set up distribution collectives such as food co-ops. It is doubtful that the desire for private property is one everybody has. If people thought that factories and supermarkets could be collectively controlled and provide for their needs adequately, it is unlikely that very many of them would still be dissatisfied until they personally owned them as well.

COOPERATION AND THE SURVIVAL OF THE SPECIES

According to the Marxist, selfishness, aggression and the desire for private property are not inborn in the human species but are acquired under certain circumstances and then only in differing degrees. In the Marxist view, the human species could not have survived if these sorts of attitudes were dominant. Humans as a species do not have the sharp claws and speed of the leopard or the tough hide of the elephant. Taken individually humans are quite weak. What makes human survival possible is our high degree of cooperation.

If humans were generally selfish and aggressive through all of our history, how could the species have survived? The anti-Marxist has only one answer to this question. He argues that in addition to being selfish, humans are also smart. Each figures out that in order to survive personally, he or she will have to cooperate with others, even if this means making some sacrifices. However, this theory leaves an important question unanswered, namely how did humans become smart in the first place? How did humans acquire the degree of intelligence necessary to figure out that cooperation was individually necessary? To the Marxist human intelligence did not appear magically, but developed out of language. And language developed out of the needs and habits of cooperative work. It was *in* social work that language and therefore intelligence developed. Hence, for the Marxist it is putting the cart before the horse to explain cooperation as a result of intelligence.

The best book by a Marxist, or anyone else I know of, on the subject of selfishness was written by Barrows Dunham and is called *Man Against Myth.* In this book Dunham makes an important distinction between people's desires and the conditions for satisfying them. He points out that there is nothing selfish at all about having desires, and in fact some very basic human desires require cooperation in order to be satisfied, such as sexual desires and the desire for companionship. Selfishness only arises when the conditions for the satisfaction of desires are such that some people cannot satisfy their desires unless others do not have theirs satisfied.

I say this distinction is important for two reasons. First, it suggests one more explanation for why so many people are prepared to believe that everyone is selfish. It is a puritanical tradition in many religions to hold that there is something wrong with having earthly desires. And to the extent that people are raised in puritanical religious environments, I think they believe that just having desires makes one selfish. Obviously, this is a mistake. *Some* desires (like sadistic ones) are wrong in themselves, but these are rare and usually considered psychopathic. In most cases there is nothing wrong at all with having desires. Selfishness only arises when one is prepared to satisfy one's own desires at others' expense.

17

The second reason to distinguish between desires and the conditions for satisfying them is that it changes the focus of attention from debates over human nature in general to concrete problems concerning the actual conditions under which we live. If social and economic conditions are such that people can only satisfy desires by being selfish, then shouldn't we strive to get rid of those conditions? One of these conditions is scarcity. If there is simply not enough to go around, then some people will have to suffer. The other main condition of selfishness is having an economic system based on private property, where production is privately controlled by people who are not prepared to share no matter how much they make, since they must keep making bigger and bigger profits to avoid being squeezed out of business by competition. These are both conditions that can be changed. To eliminate scarcity it is necessary to produce and distribute things in accord with people's needs rather than in accord with private profit for the few. To eliminate having an economic stake in being selfish, it is necessary to change the economic system. In short, it is necessary for working people to replace capitalism with socialism.

READINGS FOR CHAPTER TWO

K. Marx, F. Engels, *The German Ideology*. This book contains a defence of the view that human nature is part of society and history and thus changes. Part I (on Feuerbach) summarizes the main points Marx and Engels made. The entire book is available in a 1976 Moscow edition and in Volume 5 of the *Collected Works*. A shorter edition is available in New World Paperbacks, 1977.

F. Engels, "The Part Played by Labour in the Transition from Ape to Man." An essay that discusses the role of social work and the use of tools in the shaping of human nature.

The book referred to by Barrows Dunham, *Man Against Myth* (New York, Hill and Wang, 1962), is unfortunately out of print, but can be found in major libraries.

Chapter 3

THE FALL OF CAPITALISM

In a capitalist system the factories, mines and other major means of production are privately owned by people who employ others to do the actual work of producing "commodities" — products made not to be used by the producer but just to be sold. It was not Marx who discovered that the interests of workers and the interests of capitalists are opposed to one another in this system. Long before Marx was born working people knew that their bosses would pay as little as possible in wages and squeeze as much work as they could out of their employees.

What Marx did was to study capitalism in its historical and social contexts to discover its strengths and its weaknesses. By this study he was able to show that capitalism was not accidental, but arose quite naturally in history; and he showed that it cannot survive. Thus Marx corrected a common error in thinking among many anti-capitalists of his time who believed that capitalism is like the devil — an unnatural moral deviation, which working people had the bad luck of suffering from. At the same time Marx listed the internal contradictions in capitalism that will lead to its downfall, in contrast to pro-capitalists who say that capitalism will last forever. In this chapter I will summarize the Marxist theory that explains why capitalism cannot survive.

The main internal contradiction of capitalism is that work is highly *social* or *collectivized*, while ownership is *private*. Under capitalism most people do not work alone or in small groups to produce things for private use or to trade for things made by others. People work in groups of hundreds or thousands, using sophisticated technology to mass produce commodities. This is a very powerful economic force. How production is organized has long-range effects on the whole of a society. To be effectively and beneficially used, modern "socialized" labour needs long-range, coordinated planning. But under capitalism the people who decide what and how much to produce, where to sell, how many to hire and fire, and so on, have very short-range interests — maintaining their private profits. The result is that the mighty force of modern industry is often used against the interests of the majority of people in the form of inflation, unemployment, overproduction, underproduction, useless and faulty goods, and so on. When economic crises occur, some of the smaller capitalists themselves are driven out of business.

To understand this contradiction better it is necessary to introduce some concepts of Marxist economic theory. There are many good summaries of Marxist economics, some of which are listed at the end of this chapter. Here I will summarize only two points in order to explain why capitalism must fall.

THE LABOUR THEORY OF VALUE

Since ancient times economic theorists have been puzzled by the question of why things can be exchanged for one another, or for particular amounts of money. Why is it that you can buy a pair of shoelaces, for instance, for approximately the same amount of money that you can buy a package of chewing gum, but not for anywhere near the amount of money you would need for a car? What determines the "exchange value" of commodities?

In the Middle Ages there was a theory of the "just price." Everything had a price set by God. By the eighteenth century, when the science of economics was first developed, this theory was generally rejected. It did not explain how the Deity decided what the just price of everything was. Also economists of that period felt that the medieval church, which was itself a major economic power, used the theory in a less than disinterested way when it interpreted "just prices."

Another theory was that commodities were exchanged according to the amount of gold they could be traded for. This didn't explain how gold received its value or why some things were exchanged for more gold than others. A more recent theory suggested that things become more valuable or less valuable according to how badly people want them and how easy they are to get. If people want something because they badly need it and it is in short supply, they will be prepared to pay more for it and its value will rise. If people don't want something or if it is easy to obtain, then they will pay less, and its value will fall.

Marxists hold that this theory, called the theory of "supply and demand" helps explain the exact price something sells for in a particular time and place, but it still does not explain why things have the exchange values they do. Shoelaces always sell for less than cars, no matter how badly people want either and no matter what their supply. The theory also puts the cart before the horse, since one of the factors that affects how much people want things is how *valuable* those things are.

The theory of value Marx and Engels adopted was developed in the eighteenth century by the Scottish economic theorist, Adam Smith. It is called the "labour theory of value." According to this theory the exchange value of commodities is determined by the amount of labour, measured in working hours, necessary to make them (given current levels of technology). Shoelaces sell for less than cars, because it takes fewer people working fewer hours to make a pair of shoelaces than it does to make a car. Or, to put it another way, in the same period of time a person can make many more shoelaces than the same person could make cars. Adam Smith and other economists tested this theory by comparing prices of commodities with the necessary labour time involved in producing them. They found that while it does not explain the exact price of things, it does explain why they exchange for their approximate prices.

This theory takes the mystery out of the concept of value by relating exchange value to human labour. The value of a commodity is not some mysterious quality, but a characteristic it has in virtue of its relation to the work process that gives rise to it. Most of the early advocates of the labour theory of value were pro-capitalists, who were mainly concerned with using the theory to aid the fight against restrictions on trade and manufacture. Marx wished to deepen the theory to make it useful in working-class struggle.

THE THEORY OF SURPLUS VALUE

The economic system of capitalism is organized around the capitalist drive for private profit. Once it was understood that the value of a commodity came from the amount of labour in it, Marx asked the question: where does profit come from? A capitalist can start with some raw materials, machines and employees, then manufacture commodities and sell them. And after paying wages and costs of materials and machines, he ends up with more money than he started with. How can this be? Various attempts by pro-capitalists to answer this question have failed. The popular view that profit comes from buying cheap and selling dear does not explain where capitalist profits come from. On the buying cheap and selling dear view, the one who gains through buying cheap does so because someone else loses either through selling cheap or buying dear. If a whole economy is taken into account, losses would, therefore, cancel out gains. The theory does not explain how capitalists acquire the money necessary to invest in production in the first place or how their profits continue to grow.

Marx's answer was that profit is possible because the capitalist pays less for the labour power of the workers he hires than they produce in commodity value. A worker sells his "labour power" — his ability to work measured in time — to a capitalist for wages. But the wages received for a certain number of hours of work represent a quantity of exchange value considerably less than the exchange value of the commodities produced during those same hours. For example, an auto-worker may receive 40 dollars for eight-hours labour, but he may have produced engine parts totalling 90 dollars in value during the same period of time.

A worker's labour power is itself a commodity, which he or she sells to a capitalist in exchange for wages. The cost of this commodity is approximately what it costs to "reproduce" the worker's labour power itself. It is the cost of what is necessary to keep the worker alive, working and able to raise children who will be the next generation of workers. This cost is lower than the market cost of what is produced by that worker. (In North America today, Marxist economists estimate that the value of commodities produced is well over twice the value expressed by wages received for producing them.)

Marxists call the difference between these two amounts "surplus value." It is simply taken by the capitalist and used for things like paying rent or interest, investing in his own or other enterprises, and for his own survival and entertainment. The process of taking surplus value is called capitalist "exploitation." This process is at the heart of the capitalist economic system. Pro-capitalist economists from Marx's time to the present have expended tremendous energy trying to discredit this theory. Most of their arguments attempt to show that capitalists themselves create their profits.

Some people say that capitalists contribute to production by doing the "brain work" of management. One problem with this is that capitalists do not have to do any work (by brain or hand) if they don't want to, since they can hire people to do it. Moreover, the "brain work" that capitalists or their highly paid managers do most often does not contribute to the actual creation of commodities, but involves scheming ways to market goods, squeeze labour, or out-maneuver competition. Even if a capitalist did perform some useful function in production, his contribution to the finished product would be just that of one person among hundreds or thousands, whose combined and coordinated labours are all necessary.

Some say that capitalists derive their profits from the *risks* they have to take. This often-repeated claim has never had any weight. The mere fact of risk-taking does not create any exchange value, which is the same whether risks are taken or not. Usually, those who talk about the risks capitalists are supposed to take mean not that the risk creates value, but that because of taking risks, the capitalist deserves profits. In the first place, the Marxist theory of exploitation, as we shall see, is not a moral theory about who deserves what. But even if it were, why should risk-taking make one deserve profits? If the same goods could be produced more efficiently in a planned, socialist economy, without risking someone's individual investment, then the fact that capitalists defend a system where somebody has to take these supposed risks shows that they are either selfish or stupid, not that they deserve profits. Finally, what the capitalist presumably risks is his original investment in a means of production. But this investment itself had to come from some place. It usually represents the profits gained by somebody, and therefore has its source in the surplus value created by labour.

CAPITALIST PRODUCTION

Of course there is much more to Marxist economic theory, but this summary of capitalist exploitation will serve to show how Marx analyzed the unsolvable problem capitalism faces. A common misinterpretation of Marx's analysis is that he thought capitalism would fall because it is not fair or just. Now while Marx's discovery of the source of profit does explain the truth behind a long-standing socialist view that "capitalism is theft," Marx did not hold that capitalism would fall because it is unfair. It will fall because the capitalist system itself creates problems it cannot solve.

The production of commodities for profit is possible only when labour is collectivized. That is, it requires that a great number of people do specialized jobs using advanced machinery so as to produce the most goods in the least time. The constant pressure of competition ensures that capitalists cannot lag behind in the production of commodities. It also ensures that they must strive to keep wages down as far as possible. They lay workers off whenever keeping them on cuts into profits. (This is doubly advantageous to them, since having unemployed workers around is a threat to other workers and helps to keep wage demands down.) They also keep prices up as high as they can get away with, even *above* their exchange value if possible. These things are obviously not in the interests of working people.

There are other problems. Working people are the ones who produce commodities, but they are also the main consumers. However, since working people are not paid enough to purchase all they produce (and capitalists cannot consume what is left without cutting into profits), there are regular crises of "overproduction," where there are too many goods on the market compared to people's ability to pay for them. In extreme cases these crises become depressions. In less extreme cases they are now called "recessions," such as the protracted one we have been experiencing in Canada. An important discovery of Marx was that these crises are not accidents or the result of bad management, but are a natural outcome of the capitalist system.

Crises are marked by a general dropping off of production, with resulting layoffs and the bankruptcy of smaller capitalist firms. In the early stages of capitalism these crises often led to a drop in prices, though this did not help working people, since they also led to higher unemployment and lower wages. More recently, capitalists have learned to dampen some of the effects of crises through things like unemployment insurance. But in another way crises today are more severe than earlier ones, since they are marked by *both* growing unemployment *and* rising prices. This is due primarily to the fact that giant monopolies today are in a better position to price fix than before. Marx predicted that these crises would occur at about ten-year intervals and that the intervals would grow shorter as capitalism nears its end. His predictions are proving correct.

Many other problems are created by the capitalist economy, and the ones I have mentioned have many more facets. Those who wish to pursue these topics might want to read one of the several Marxist texts on the subject or read Marx's famous *Capital*, where the mechanics of the capitalist economic system are discussed in detail.

Marx described capitalist production as "anarchy." This does not mean that individual capitalists are crazy or irrational, but that the entire system, motivated as it is by competition for private profit, creates more problems than it can solve. In talking about the anarchy of capitalist production, Marx was contrasting it to what he saw would be possible in a socialist, planned economy where collectivized mass production is organized so as to serve the best long-range interests of the working people themselves. In socialist economies there are no economic crises, and needless to say there are no policies to create unemployment or keep wages down. Under a system of private ownership, this sort of planning has no place.

THE WORKING CLASS

The working class is made up of those people who do not own any means of production but sell their ability to work to those who do. The most important conclusion Marx drew from his analysis of capitalism is that it is the working class that can and will lead successful socialist revolutions. In this view, Marxists differ from those who see socialist revolutions led by a few individuals, or as a rising of all groups in society against capitalism without any group playing a leading role, or as the result of capitalists themselves becoming "enlightened" and handing over power. The contradiction between collectivized labour and private ownership is expressed as the contradiction between capitalists and the working class.

The system of capitalist commodity production brings the working class into existence. But in doing so, capitalism also creates a force that eventually destroys the capitalist system itself. As Marx and Engels put it, capitalism creates its own "grave diggers." The Marxist basis for this view is that because of its mode of work, the working class is provided with both the *ability* to lead a successful revolution and also the *incentive* to want one.

Workers have the incentive to change the social and economic system of capitalism for several reasons. Even working people with relatively high wages cannot afford the luxuries taken for granted by capitalists and their overpaid managers. In a system geared to private profit, life for most working people is hard. Apart from monotonous, tiring and unrewarding work, workers face the constant pressure of job insecurity. One's old age is not adequately provided for. A working person has practically no say in the safety of his or her work conditions, much less in how work is organized or what is produced.

Through work, working-class people also acquire the ability to change this oppressive system. Industrialization forced people off farms and out of small shops and into cities and large factories. Industrialized work creates the habits and skills of collectivity and discipline. Knowing how to work consistently in a coordinated way does not come automatically to people. Depending on their class background and type of job, some never learn these things. Large-scale industries and offices train workers in these skills. These are potentially revolutionary abilities. The main force standing in the way of socialism is the capitalist class, which is small in number but controls weighty instruments of power, such as the army and the police. To compensate for this advantage, the rest of society must be able to move in a collective, united and disciplined way.

Through its regular work, there is another advantage gained by the working class. At least in its industrial sector, the class has its hands on the actual means of production. It has the ability to stop the wheels of production and also to turn them on again. Not only do workers have some direct power over the capitalists, but they learn that they can challenge capitalists and make gains in their own interests. This is important, because capitalists try to make working people feel powerless and unsure of themselves.

Early in its history the working class learned that it has these abilities and strengthened them through the formation of unions. The value of working-class unity and collectivity makes itself felt when workers cooperate in strikes, refuse to cross picket lines or support other issues. These skills are crucial to winning a revolution and building a socialist society. And the working class learns them in a kind of on-the-job training program unwittingly provided under capitalism.

The Marxist view about the central revolutionary role of the working class has come under fire from several directions. One criticism is that the peasantry is the key revolutionary class. Another is that the working class has "sold out." We will look at these criticisms in turn.

Peasants and industrial workers. Russia and China had large peasant populations, that is, poor farmers whose families used almost all they produced. More recently peasants and landless farmworkers have been active in third-world liberation struggles. These facts have led some to conclude that Marx and Engels were wrong to see industrial workers as the key to revolutionary change. They claim instead that peasants play the crucial role of leading the fight for socialism.

I suppose the effect of accepting this view in Canada would be that we must watch peasants liberate other parts of the world, since there is no peasant class to speak of in Canada. However, even in parts of the world where there are sizable numbers of peasants, the theory is flawed. This is not to say that there is no grain of truth in it. Marxists have taken a closer look at the important role of the peasantry since Marx's time. But the view that the working class has ceased to play a leading revolutionary role in certain parts of the world is wrong.

Jack Woddis, a Communist exile from South Africa, has written an excellent book, *New Theories of Revolution,* in which he criticizes advocates of this view, such as Franz Fanon and Regis Debray. Woddis examines most of South America and Africa and shows how militant working-class activity has often been instrumental in initiating struggles for national liberation. In his study of African struggles from the late 1940s to the present, he concludes:

> In country after country the workers acted as pace makers of the national liberation struggle. They staged major confrontations with imperialism, organized strike struggles, most of which were fought with great tenacity and courage, sacrificed in prison and in front of the bullets of the imperialist troops, and helped to awaken the entire nation. General strikes became manifestations of national struggle and stirred millions into an awareness of the total system of colonial oppression and discrimination, of the necessity to fight against it, and of the possibility of defeating it.

Another problem with the concept of peasant leadership is that it overlooks some very important additions to the theory of Marxism since it was first advanced over a century ago. The most important of these concerns *imperialism.* In the late nineteenth century and throughout the twentieth century, industrialized capitalist countries such as England, the United States, France, Japan and others began wholesale capitalist expansion into other parts of the world. Either by direct military invasion or by installing puppet governments, they forced large parts of the world to provide cheap labour and raw materials for them and to serve as a captive market for manufactured goods at inflated prices.

Africa, Asia, South and Central America, Russia and Eastern

Europe were quite consciously divided up by the big industrial powers. The economic gains were great and in some cases almost certainly staved off revolutions at home by bailing out the home economy and stemming discontent. (Canada has found itself in the unique position of being both subject to imperialism, first by England and now by the U.S., and at the same time acting as an imperialist country itself, particularly in the Caribbean.)

The effect of imperialism on non-industrialized parts of the world was to create revolutionary potential there. In some places imperialism introduced a measure of heavy industry, which created the beginnings of a militant industrial working class. But even in those countries where little industry was developed the nature of farm work itself began to change as peasants were forced to become farmworkers on large plantations owned by other people, usually European colonial settlers. This created another economic shift as small-scale, variety crop production gave way to large-scale single commodity production (of such products as coffee, tobacco or sugar).

Earlier I suggested that incentive and the ability to change the system were qualities of the industrial working class that make it the key force in revolutionary change. Where peasant forces have been instrumental in revolutionary movements it is because imperialism has forged similar qualities in them. The peasantry does the work; someone else makes the profit. Agricultural and plantation work in imperialized countries is highly collectivized and disciplined. The point is that where peasant forces play a revolutionary role this is not because Marx and Engels were wrong about the revolutionary nature of the working class, but because imperialism has created some important working-class qualities in the peasantry.

Has the working class "sold out"? The North American media have created the image of the industrial worker as a bloated and complacent person who has a stake in maintaining the present social system. This image has prompted some to suggest that while the working class may have had revolutionary potential in the 1930s, it has now been "bought off" and has chosen instead to support capitalism. There are two questions here: Is the working class bloated? And has it sold out?

If someone measures a person's well-being against a standard of complete poverty — starvation, rags for clothing, no roof over one's head — then I suppose that most North American industrial workers are well off. But this is not a realistic standard. Well-being should be measured against what is possible. In a land rich in natural resources and industrial potential, it is not necessary for working people to have to pay from 25 per cent to 50 per cent of their income on housing. Inflation should not make each year's paycheck worth less than before. Even with a high-paying job, how well off is someone if that job could be taken away at any time? In fact only some working people have high-paying jobs. According to government statistics, around 25 per cent of Canadian families live below the poverty line (8,000 dollars per year).

The view that the working class has sold out is heard more in North America than in other parts of the world. In Europe working people in countries like France and Italy swell the ranks of revolutionary parties that may be on the eve of transforming those countries to socialism. What is the difference between the working classes of those countries and of Canada or the U.S.? On the "sell-out" theory the difference must be that the North American worker is too cowardly or too stupid or too immoral to risk leading society in revolutionary change.

Marxists maintain that this theory rests on a wrong view about how people come to have the attitudes they do. It supposes that at some point members of the North American working class came to the realization that socialism is an alternative and revolution requires working-class leadership, but then they deliberately chose to turn their backs on socialism.

Revolutionary consciousness and determination do not come and go in such a haphazard fashion. It is not a matter of an effort of will. To think that having or abandoning revolutionary consciousness is a matter of individual choice is to view things in a narrowly moralistic way. Sometimes I suspect that people who hold the sell-out theory confuse worker militancy in strikes with *revolutionary* militancy: since North American workers are quite militant trade unionists, it is assumed that they must also be revolutionaries. Then when they don't organize in large numbers for revolution, the conclusion is drawn that they have sold out.

There are definite conditions that lead to revolutionary consciousness. These include economic conditions, the effectiveness of anti-revolutionary propaganda, the nature and extent of working-class political organizations, the success of divide-and-conquer tactics, and so on. Largely because of the success of imperialism, important sectors of the North American working class were spared the worst economic pressures, and this meant that they did not look for solutions to their problems outside of the capitalist

29

system. This has, indeed, been one of the many bad effects of imperialism. The task of the scientific socialist, however, is not to berate working people for not being revolutionary, but to discover just what conditions lead to revolution and what conditions hold it back.

CAN CAPITALISM BE SAVED?

To summarize, the Marxist claim is that capitalism has created economic forces it cannot control, much less direct for the benefit of everybody in society. At the same time capitalism has brought into existence the modern working class, which *can* control and direct those forces. But it can only do so by a socialist transformation of society, which ends the system of capitalist exploitation altogether. Thus capitalism digs its own grave.

Some people maintain that while this may have been true of the "classic" capitalism Marx was writing about, capitalism has now changed in ways that make it stronger, and capitalists have taken measures to aviod socialist revolution. Thus, they say that capitalism can be saved. Marxists do not deny that capitalism has changed and that capitalists use their considerable power to fight socialism. However, the internal problems of capitalism cannot be overcome in the long run, and measures taken to avoid socialism can only set it back temporarily. I will conclude this chapter by looking at five things that are often said to be able to save capitalism.

Imperialism. We have already noted that advanced capitalism turns into its imperialist phase. By forcing people in other parts of the world to work at starvation wages, capitalists increased profits and were able to yield to some of the workers' demands in their home country for higher wages. By creating captive markets in other countries, capitalists had places to sell goods at inflated prices and to dump goods when there were crises of overproduction at home.

Does imperialism, then, save capitalism? Some have maintained that it does. They note that Marx and Engels predicted a probable socialist revolution in England or Germany in the last century. But due to imperialist ventures, these revolutions did not take place, and hence, it is argued, Marx's whole theory is shown to be false. The failure of this prediction has shown that there were inadequacies in the theory, but it did not show that the theory is wrong. Lenin wrote an important book on this subject called *Imperialism, the Highest Stage of Capitalism* in which he shows how imperialism is a natural outgrowth of capitalism — one that does

30

temporarily solve some problems, but that can only postpone revolutions in the major capitalist countries, not prevent them.

The difficulty imperialism created was to move the problems of capitalism to new territory. In fact it moves it to territory less advantageous to the capitalists. By super-exploiting workers in countries subject to imperialist rule, it creates even greater incentive for revolution. Imperialism also sparks nationalistic sentiments. At home imperialists can flag wave and urge their own working class to go along with them for the sake of their common country (a cynical ploy, since capitalists don't care about the real needs of their countries). In the nations they subject to imperialist plunder, capitalists are correctly regarded as foreign invaders who have no business there at all. Imperialism has made it relatively easy for forces of national liberation and revolution, such as the NLF in Vietnam, to rally large segments of the population to the anti-imperialist struggle.

Taking imperialism into account, Lenin predicted that capitalism, regarded on a worldwide scale, would snap first at its "weakest link," which he considered his own native Russia. The Russia of that time was both an imperialist power, caught up in a costly and destructive war between imperialist rivals for markets (World War I), and at the same time it was subject to the imperialist domination by stronger capitalist countries. Taking these factors into account, it should not be surprising that the first socialist revolution was in Russia and the other nations that make up the USSR. Similarly, China, Cuba, North Korea and, for the most part, the countries of Eastern Europe, all of which are now socialist, were subject to the most devastating imperialist rule. It is because of imperialism also that national-liberation struggles in Africa, Latin America and Asia often move quickly in a socialist direction.

Monopolization. Competition is a major source of capitalist economic problems. Why cannot capitalists eliminate competition through creating monopolies? Monopolization has indeed helped many capitalists. Groups of capitalist concerns form monopolies (or, what comes to the same thing, "cartels" or "conglomerates") that fix prices and remove some of the pressure of competition. Every time there is an economic crisis, smaller capitalist enterprises go under, leaving larger and larger ones to corner the market even further.

Still, monopolization will not save capitalism. In the first place, like imperialism, it creates special problems of its own for the capitalist system. Capitalist ownership of the means of production

31

cannot become concentrated in fewer hands without more and more smaller capitalists going out of business. This has the effect of forcing more discontented people into the working class, and it makes it harder to maintain the myth that anybody with enough intelligence and drive can be a capitalist.

Theoretically, I suppose one could imagine a single world monopoly which could afford to pay higher wages and improve working conditions, because it had no fear of competitors who by keeping wages down would be able to produce competitive products for less. But think of how unlikely such a development really is. It would not be enough for some capitalists to gain a monopoly in just one industry. They would have to monopolize *all* industries. If someone monopolized the entire auto industry and then stopped making improvements in auto-manufacturing machines, what is to prevent an enterprising manufacturer in some other industry from using his profits to invest in new and better auto-making machines, thus becoming a competitor of the auto monopoly? This sort of industry jumping is not at all unusual in capitalism.

Not only would capitalists have to monopolize all industries; they would have to monopolize the whole world. Capitalists do not care about state boundaries. They are prepared to make profits wherever they can manufacture goods the cheapest and sell them at the highest prices. But even if this imaginary world monopoly *could* have been created, it is now too late, because capitalists have to contend with competition from the socialist countries, which do not have economic crises and are becoming more and more economically powerful each year.

In the U.S., where monopolization has developed quite far, there is still vicious rivalry among *different* groups of large capitalists, who still have all the characteristics that mark the anarchy of capitalist production. Monopolization is only beneficial to some capitalists in the short run. And it does not change the fact that modern production has outgrown a private-profit economy. The dream (or nightmare) of a single world monopoly is so far from reality that it is hardly worth considering.

State involvement. In the early days of capitalism, most pro-capitalists argued that the government ought to play a very small role in the economy. At that time they wanted to break the government-church-feudal network which had attempted to constrain manufacture and trade. Now, even if they pay lip service to this philosophy, the largest capitalists all promote active government involvement in the economy. This is because they see that governments can help them to weather crises and make profits. In some capitalist countries the government plays a larger role than in others, but in all capitalist countries, government involvement in the economy is on the increase.

Pro-capitalist governments help ease crises by making loans and tax gifts to businesses and by controlling wages. They purchase expensive goods, such as military equipment, from corporations at inflated prices. They help corporations to market their goods. For instance, the Canadian government helps Canadian-based war-goods producers to market their wares through the Canadian Commercial Corporation (a Crown corporation formerly called "War Supplies Limited.")

Pro-capitalist governments finance the research for new technology, which is then used by capitalists in production. Sometimes governments run some industries for the capitalists. Occasionally people talk of countries like England as if they were socialist because the government owns and runs some major industries (such as the English coal industry). In fact, some essential industries are no longer profitable, so the government manages these industries for the capitalists.

Useful as state regulation of portions of the economy can be for capitalists, it cannot save the system of capitalism. The main problem is that the government has to find the money to do all these things somewhere. If government projects were financed by the capitalists, their profits would fall, which is just what government involvement in the economy is supposed to prevent. Therefore all capitalist governments leave giant loopholes in their corporation tax structures, and the state gets its money from working people. But higher taxes just create more discontent and further lower people's ability to purchase goods.

State regulation of the economy in the interests of capitalists has a two-edged effect on people's attitudes toward government. On the one hand, by trading on the capitalist-inspired myth that any government regulation is a form of socialism, it confuses people about what socialism is and makes them cynical. If this is socialism, who needs it? On the other hand, it opens the door to some economic reforms that people can force the government to make. For instance, working people can force the government to enact legislation setting minimum wages or regulating working conditions, which they could not do if the government played no role in economic matters at all. Even if these reforms are minor, relative to people's needs, they help them to learn what *could* be done if there was a workers' government that ran the entire economy in their own interests.

Threats of violence. A time-honoured method of oppressive regimes is to try keeping people down by threatening them with job loss, prison or even death if they try anything revolutionary. Capitalism is no exception. During the 1919 Winnipeg General Strike, which was put down with horses, clubs and guns, workers learned that capitalists are prepared to use police against the people. The lesson has been repeated many times in Canadian working-class history. How far can the threat of jail or harassment go in preventing people from challenging the capitalist system?

Obviously threats have some effect. Any sane person thinks twice before taking risks. But I do not think that threats of violence can save capitalism any more than they have saved any of the oppressive systems that preceded it. If history has taught us nothing else, it has taught us that there are limits to how far people can be bullied. Look at situations where the threats and actual use of violence have been extreme.

Portuguese people lived under the systematic terror of fascism for 48 years. Now we learn that the Communist Party there was actively organizing underground the whole time at tremendous risk and had a membership of around 30,000 just before the 1974 anti-fascist coup.

I heard a priest from the U.S. who had been locked up in the prisons of Vietnam tell of Vietnamese women who were brought out every morning and told that if they didn't salute the U.S. flag and the flag of its puppet government, they would be beaten and then put into the infamous "tiger cages" (rooms about four feet square, some of which were made in Canada). He reported that almost to a woman they refused to salute those symbols of imperialism. There is a point where human dignity rebels at the brutality of intimidation.

Mind control. Through the school system and the pro-capitalist news and entertainment media, working people are subjected to a daily barrage of propaganda designed to convince them that capitalism is good, that socialism is evil, that you can't change things, that the real source of your problems is the working people of another race or

34

nationality or sex, or that you, yourself, are to blame for your problems. There are any number of other ideas designed to confuse working people about what is wrong and how to change things. Of course, many people in educational and cultural institutions are themselves honestly confused about the source of their problems and pass on the theories they have learned. Nevertheless, such propaganda dampens revolutionary class consciousness and hence helps to perpetuate capitalism.

Effective as capitalist mind-control techniques are, there are limits to how long they can save capitalism. People who have already participated in socialist revolutions were all subjected to pro-capitalist propaganda, as were the working people and their allies all over the capitalist world who are now engaged in anti-capitalist struggles. Why cannot others overcome the effects of this propaganda too? It is typical of the elitist thinking of the bourgeoisie to regard working people as fools and sheep who can be convinced of anything. In fact, life itself has a way of revealing truths and exposing lies.

READINGS FOR CHAPTER THREE

K. Marx, *Capital.* This major work is available in different editions, both paperback and hardback. Volume One contains the main outline of Marx's theory.

K. Marx, "Wages, Price and Profit"; "Wage Labour and Capital." Two short articles on some aspects of Marx's economic views written for workers' education.

F. Engels, *Anti-Dühring,* Chapter II, sections v-ix. These sections of Engels' criticism of a contemporary anti-Marxist socialist (Dühring) contain a good summary of Marxist economic theory.

V.I. Lenin, *Imperialism, the Highest Stage of Capitalism* (in Volume 22 of the *Collected Works).* Lenin's application and development of Marxism to account for imperialism.

There are many Marxist economists who have written books explaining and defending Marxist theories. My favourite author is Maurice Dobb. He has written one summary of Marxist economics on an introductory level, *Marx As an Economist* (London, Lawrence & Wishart, 1943, reprinted 1975), and several more advanced ones, including *Political Economy and Capitalism* (London, Routledge & Kegan Paul, 1940) which defends Marxism against modern bourgeois critics.

The Jack Woddis book referred to on page 27 is *New Theories of Revolution* (New York, New World Paperbacks, 1972, reprinted 1974).

Chapter 4

HISTORICAL MATERIALISM

With the exception of the idle rich, people must work to stay alive. In this way humans are like other animals. However, humans differ from other animals in the *way* they work and in the *effects* they have on nature and on themselves in the process. Lacking the sharp claws, tough hides or other natural equipment that make the survival of other species possible, humans use their hands and their brains to make *tools* and they work *socially*, by dividing up the jobs that need to be done. Some other animals use simple tools (for instance, some birds use sticks to dig bugs out of tree bark), and there are animals that have a simple division of labour as when male lions drive prey into areas where female lions are lying in wait for them. But no animal other than humans can produce even such a simple tool as a bow and arrow, let alone a steamship or a modern factory. Even early human societies contained a greater division of labour than is found among other animals — some hunted while others planted, wove, made pots, and so on. Of course there is nothing at all in the world of other animals to compare with the highly complex division of labour of modern societies.

The effect of this division of labour and use of tools has been that humans not only survived but produced more than was necessary for one generation to stay alive. Hence, each generation of humans has left behind it more than it started with. Using this surplus, people could be freed to do different kinds of labour, to acquire different skills and to develop new tools, so the division of labour and technological development became more and more complex. The production of a surplus has had another effect as well.

It has made it possible for some people not to work at all, but to live off the labour of those who do work.

These facts about the nature of human work are central to the Marxist theory of history — "historical materialism." It is a general scientific theory that guides Marxists in their efforts to understand the past and to change the present. Among other things, this theory explains why it is no accident that capitalism has bred the problems discussed in chapter three. It explains how capitalism came into existence in the first place, and why it is now being replaced by socialism.

To study anything scientifically it is necessary to *classify* the subject matter and to *explain* what goes on in that subject matter by discovering laws of its behaviour. Neither classifications nor laws are easy to find. They do not "jump out" of a subject matter, so to speak, and reveal themselves to a scientist, but have to be discovered by much careful investigation. For instance, it took the science of chemistry well over a century to discover the classifications of chemical elements and the laws of chemical combination that we learn in high-school chemistry classes today. In a similar way Marx and Engels had to study the process of human history carefully and learn from both the correct insights and the mistakes of previous thinkers — as well as examining the practical struggles of their own times — before they could formulate the basic tenets of historical materialism. They took as their starting place the social use of tools by humans.

MODE OF PRODUCTION

The basic Marxist category within human societies is the "mode of production." This category is made up of two things: the "forces of production" and the "relations of production." The forces of production include such things as tools and machines, systems of transport, factory buildings and warehouses, land, sources of energy and raw materials — in short, the "means of production." Of course the forces of production also include the working people themselves who use these means of production to transform nature into products suitable for human use. In early society the means of production were simple — hammers, crude plows and so on. In more complex societies they include sophisticated things like modern factories or power plants.

The "relations of production" refer most importantly to the

division in a society between those who own its means of production and those who do not own any means of production and are therefore obliged to work for those who do, to stay alive. This is the *class* division between owners and workers.

Economic classes. An "economic class" is a group of people who share a common relation to the means of production. The "ruling class" owns the key means of production in a society. Owning these means, they are able to compel others to work for them and to take the fruits of this work for themselves. In the last chapter we discussed two classes — the capitalists and the working class. The capitalist class, also called the "bourgeoisie," includes those who privately own and control the major means of production in an economy based on mass producing commodities. Private owners of large means of distribution and of the banks and other major financial institutions are also considered parts of the capitalist class by most Marxists. These three sectors of the capitalist class closely interact and there is much overlap in their membership. An earlier ruling class was made up of feudal lords, who owned farmland (either directly or as agents of a king) that was worked by "serfs." Still earlier there were "slave-holders" who, among other things, owned other people.

The "working class" or "proletariat" is made up of those people who do not own any means of production but must work for people who do. Sometimes Marxists use "proletariat" to mean only the industrial working class, or those whose work is most directly related to the production of surplus value, as that term was defined in the last chapter. Factory workers, miners, transport and construction workers and others engaged in large-scale production and distribution fall into this category. Their work makes them the most highly disciplined segment of the working class with the most experience in organizing against the effects of capitalism. Members of the industrial working class tend to form the core of revolutionary political parties in industrialized societies.

In addition to the industrial working class, there are service workers, clerical workers and many others. Their labour is less directly related to the creation of surplus value; however, as capitalism develops they are increasingly forced into regimented work similar to that of the industrial working class. Changes in technology have also affected industrial work by demanding more skills of industrial workers and by requiring closer coordination between work in factories and work outside them. Because of these changes the industrial working class has grown and diversified its modes of work, and it has been able to find more and more allies among other segments of the working class.

Under capitalism not everyone is either a member of the capitalist class or of the proletariat. Marx and Engels noted several other groups and classes. There are those people who privately own a small means of production or distribution which they must work themselves or with the help of their families or a few employees in order to make a profit. These members of the "petty-bourgeoisie" include people who own small businesses, shopkeepers and family farmers who own their own farms. There are also people sometimes called members of the "middle class," like lawyers, doctors, professional engineers and people who work in corporations as middle management. Some of these people are self-employed, but even when they work for salaries, their work is not as highly organized as that of the working class and they usually make more money. Also, they are often hired to supervise other employees and increase productivity.

Some people in the petty-bourgeoisie and from the middle class realize that it is in their interests to line up with the working class against capitalists. In fact some have no choice, since the economic squeeze created by the domination of a few large monopoly capitalist interests hurts them as well as the working class and forces some of them into the working class. Others from these groups throw in their lot with the capitalists, as do some of the chronically unemployed and down and out (the "lumpen-proletariat"). In Canada, farmers often, but not always, line up with city workers against capitalism.

Historical materialists do not present their categories as a complete classification of absolutely everything that can be found in human society. They do present their classifications as representing groups and relationships which actually exist in society and which are the most important for understanding and changing things. As with the classifications of any scientific theory, there are borderline cases where it is not clear which class a person fits into, but the general meanings of Marxist classifications are clear enough. These meanings must be kept in mind to avoid confusion. Owning a house or a car does not make someone a capitalist. For this you need to own something like a factory and employ people to create surplus value for you. A capitalist who chooses to work in his own factory or bank, as some do in a management capacity, does not therefore become a worker. He does not have to work unless he wants to, and his economically central role is as an owner and employer.

Those, then, are the components of a society's mode of production: its forces of production and its relations of production. The mode of production is often called the "economic base" of society by historical materialists. Societies also include political institutions — the government and the courts, with systems of law and agencies like the army and the police to enforce them. And, in every society there are ideas: philosophical ideas, morality, religion, cultural and scientific views. Historical materialists call all these institutions and ideas the "superstructure" of society. Political institutions are the "political" or "legal-political" part of the superstructure, while the main systems of ideas are referred to as its "ideological super-structure." (Sometimes the word "ideology" is used more narrowly by Marxists to describe just some of the leading ideas of a society, namely those unscientific ideas which only serve to rationalize oppressive rule.)

LAWS OF HISTORICAL MATERIALISM

Marxist social scientists have discovered many laws of social development, some more general than others. Here I will summarize two of the most general laws of historical materialism. First, by and large, a society's superstructure is determined by its economic base. Specifically, in a class-divided society the type of existing political system is determined by the needs of that society's ruling class, and the dominant ideas of the society are for the most part the ideas of its ruling class.

This finding is disputed by practically all anti-Marxist social scientists, and Marxism is denounced as crude and simplistic for advancing it, but some reflection should convince anyone that it is correct. People must work to stay alive, and it would be most strange if the tools used and the social relations guiding this work did not shape the rest of society. Surely it is no accident that complex governmental forms and scientific theories like those of modern physics did not appear in ancient times. As each and every seventeenth- and eighteenth-century European society began to change its methods of production to ones with capitalist relations of production, similar changes followed in the country's type of government. Parliamentary governments were formed (which, as we will see, are best suited to capitalist interests), and the dominant philosophical ideas changed from medieval religious views to ones favouring scientific invention and economic competition.

The other main law of historical materialism is that major changes within a society's mode of production are caused by conflicts between its forces and relations of production. In very early societies, where hunters and gatherers used simple tools, there were no class divisions. This was not because people in these societies, called "primitive communism" by Marx and Engels, were believers in socialist theory, but simply because there was very little division of labour and the economy was not sophisticated enough for anyone to privately hoard a surplus. The forces of production in early societies were mainly human hands and brains aided by very simple tools. The relations of production were equally simple — little division of labour and no ruling class.

There are ongoing debates among Marxist anthropologists over the nature of these hunting and gathering classless societies and how they changed into class-divided ones. Following the most advanced anthropological thinking of their time, Marx and Engels seemed to have held that there were no ruling classes because life was too hard, so there was no surplus above what was needed to keep the members of a tribe alive for anyone to exploit. However, hunting and gathering work, primitive as it was, eventually led to several changes in society that undermined the early communistic nature of this mode of work itself. Contact between tribes created trade. It led to war and the taking of captives as slaves. Standing armies came into existence. Agriculture replaced hunting and gathering. With the production of a surplus for the first time, some people found themselves not hunting, farming or doing any physical labour. They found themselves also in a position to personally control new means of production and to take as their own the surplus created by the rest of their tribe. New relations of production appeared and humanity entered the period of history in which societies are torn by class division between rulers and ruled.

More recent work, by both Marxist and non-Marxist anthropologists, suggests that in most, if not all places, early hunters and gatherers did not experience want. Compared to the peasants who succeeded them, they worked fewer hours and consumed a more adequate and varied diet. What these people did lack was a technology of food preservation, that is, the ability to accumulate a surplus which would free some from the daily necessity to hunt and gather. This possibility emerged only with agriculture, when some people,

42

freed from productive labour, took personal control of agricultural land.

Whatever the various origins of class-divided society might have been, Marx and Engels noted that from the point where classes emerged history progressed differently in different parts of the world. Areas of Asia developed in one way, of Europe in another, depending on raw materials available, geography, and the specific means of production that took hold. In the history of Europe egalitarian communities gave way to large land-and-slave-holding empires. These in turn were replaced by feudalism, which was replaced by capitalism.

In each transformation the pattern was the same. Forces of production that at one time worked in relative harmony with certain relations of production outgrew them and these relations of production became fetters on developing forces. At the same time, new relations of production came into being and encouraged new productive forces. For instance, under feudalism the means of production included farm implements, crude mining and irrigational tools and relatively simple devices to aid manufacture and navigation. Ruling class feudal lords took a major portion of what was produced by farming serfs. However, with increased trade and manufacture, new classes of manufacturers and merchants emerged to develop new and profitable means of production. Geared to agriculture and simple trade, the old relations of production began to retard the development of trade and large-scale manufacture. Feudal relations gave way to new relations in which capitalists became the ruling class. They employed city workers who had left the farms (forming an industrial proletariat) and developed the tremendous potential of new technology. These changes in the relations of production were accompanied by political developments in which bourgeois revolutions (all of them involving violence) replaced feudal states with capitalist-dominated ones.

World capitalism now faces a situation where the productive forces that it developed have outgrown capitalist relations of production. Industrialized production has become too massive and interdependent to be run by individual competitive capitalists who are driven by the profit motive. The effects of technological changes are too long-term and too important to be guided by such short-term individual desires. In the last chapter, the contradiction between social labour and private ownership was discussed. One effect of this contradiction is the mess all capitalist economies are in. Food in one part of the world is destroyed, while in other parts of the world (or

HISTORY

even in the same country) people starve. There is chronic unemployment. Inflation continues. The gap between rich and poor widens. And social revolution occurs as working people organize to take political power and institute social ownership of the means of production.

The pattern of changing relations of production is as before, but with an important difference. For the first time it is working people themselves who are taking control of the means of production, not a small group of people who do not themselves work. A socialist transformation is one in which the majority of the people, those who do the actual work, become the ruling class. In this respect socialism marks a major turning point in history. It begins an era in which the mighty tools that humans have created can finally be used in a planned and rational way for the benefit of humanity as a whole.

In the application of the general theory of historical materialism Marxists have discovered other historical laws — despite the claim of anti-Marxist historians that there are no laws in history. Including laws we have already discussed, some of the more important laws Marxists have discovered are:

> Changes in a society's mode of production ultimately cause changes in its superstructure.
> Social revolutions result from a conflict between a society's forces of production and its relations of production.
> Capitalist mass production is a source of working-class organization and militancy.
> Advanced capitalist need for expansion leads to imperialism.
> Threatened capitalism tends toward fascism.
> Rivalry between and within economic classes causes war.

These laws are stated in a general and simplified form. To apply them, the historical materialist, like a scientist in any other field, must examine the specific features of the concrete situation. Marxists claim that their study of history has proven these and other laws correct, and they challenge anti-Marxists to provide explanations for such things as imperialism, social revolution and war that match the facts of history better than do the explanations of historical materialism.

DO MARXISTS REDUCE EVERYTHING TO ECONOMICS?

Those who charge that Marxists reduce everything to economics sometimes object to the fact that Marxists view production as central for understanding what goes on in a society. Well, Marxists view it as central because it *is* central. This is not a case of simplistic "reduction" but of recognizing the fact that, as Engels put it: "Human beings must first of all eat, drink, shelter and clothe themselves before they can turn their attention to politics, science, art and religion." Hence, it is the organization of work — the forces of production and the class relations of production — that has been the most important factor in determining the overall movement of history.

Usually the belief that Marxists reduce everything to economics comes from a misunderstanding of Marxism. Sometimes people have in mind a concept of "economics" that is much narrower than the Marxist one. They think that Marxists hold a crude theory of "technological determinism," which maintains that machines cause everything; or they think of "economics" in the same way as the bourgeois economists who typically limit it to considerations of how capitalists market goods. For Marxists, the economic base of society is much broader. However, even in the broad sense of "economic base," where this includes all a society's forces and relations of production, Marxists do not "reduce" everything to economics.

Marx and Engels never held that absolutely everything that happens in history is caused by economic factors. On the contrary, Marxists maintain that non-economic factors have important effects on a society's economy. To put this in historical-materialist terms, Marxists maintain that while what happens in the superstructure is caused by what happens in the economic base, there are also causes that work the other way. One example is the scientific discoveries that lead to the invention of new tools, or means of production.

Also, certain religious attitudes or right-wing political systems, both part of the superstructure of society, may hold back changes in the forces or relations of production. In the early days of capitalism pro-feudal religious leaders successfully prevented the use of new technology in some places, and under fascism trade union and other working-class organizational activity is made extremely difficult.

In saying that the economic base is central for social change, Marxists mean that the *overall pattern* of historical change can only be understood and predicted by looking at the changing way people work, not by looking just at the governmental forms or theories people have. Major changes in the superstructure can be made if there is a major change in the economic base, but not the other way around. Therefore, Marxists maintain that political revolutions require certain economic bases and cannot be artificially imposed. Although the superstructure can affect the base, it cannot do so unless the base is itself developed sufficiently to be affected. For instance, while scientific discoveries revolutionized industry in the eighteenth century, those same discoveries would not have had the same effect in earlier societies. In fact, the steam engine was discovered in ancient Greece, but since the forces and relations of production were too underdeveloped to convert to industrialization, it was just used as a toy by the rich.

STEAM ENGINE

SUBJECTIVISM

Another common criticism of historical materialism is that it does not take into account how people think of themselves. Anti-Marxist sociologists regularly do opinion surveys to show that while Marxists might consider all the factory workers in a country members of the proletariat, some of these workers think of themselves as middle class or maybe some even as upper class. This approach of bourgeois theorists, called "subjectivism," suggests that people are just what they think they are.

Subjectivism has never cut much ice with Marxists, who are more interested in what people really are than what they may think themselves to be. If you were to put all the people who consider themselves "middle class" in the same scientific classification, you would have to group together people who may have nothing else in common except this belief.

The subjectivist criticism of Marxism would have some weight if people *never* came to see themselves as being accurately described by the Marxist classifications. But despite what the subjectivists say, there is no wide gap between Marxist class analysis and how people think of themselves. In the first place, the sociologists' opinion surveys seldom define terms when asking people to classify themselves. If a factory worker was asked to say whether he was a member of the middle class, and "middle class" was explicitly described as being part of management or a professional such as a doctor or a lawyer, I very much doubt that he would think himself middle class by this definition.

In the second place, while some people can maintain illusions about their place in society, very few can maintain them for long. I imagine that in a small plant a factory worker might help to make some minor management decisions and even feel chummy with the boss, thus gaining the illusion of being part of management. But this attitude is hard to maintain when he is fired by his "chum" or when the boss sells the business and retires to Florida leaving his fellow "manager" to join the ranks of the unemployed.

Subjectivists also criticize Marxists for not being "humanistic." They claim that by classifying people in economic terms, Marxists cease to be concerned with people's personal, human qualities — their hopes and fears, their values and beliefs. If Marxists weren't concerned about these things, they would not work so hard to create a world where people's hopes can be realized and inhuman values like racism are not bred. But to build such a world we must figure out how the present one works, and for this we need the scientific categories that best explain it.

Thinking of people in terms of their mode of work is completely compatible with thinking of them in truly human terms. Work is the transformation of nature into humanly useful things. Human work shapes and in turn is shaped by human values and beliefs. If work becomes debasing, cold and inhuman, it is not because there is something wrong with the human transformation of nature. The problem lies with capitalist rule, where people do not work for themselves but for the private profit of those who care little about the quality of work or its effects on humans, other species and nature. Wanting to understand how this takes place in order to change it is a deeply humanistic goal.

Because anti-Marxist theorists believe it is impossible to give any general explanations of what happens in history, they have devoted much energy to trying to show that historical materialism cannot be correct. Despite the cleverness of many of their arguments, I do not believe that purely abstract arguments can settle this question. It is necessary to look at actual historical facts to decide whether they are best explained by historical materialism, or by some other theory, or whether they are explained by no theory at all. In the next chapter I will contrast historical materialism with some of the popular, non-Marxist ideas that people have about history.

READINGS FOR CHAPTER FOUR

Dynamics of Social Change, edited by H. Selsam, D. Goldway, & H. Martel (New York, New World Paperbacks, 1970, reprinted 1975). This book of selections from works of Marx, Engels, and Lenin, both explaining historical materialism and applying it, is useful as a guide to help one find works of these authors for further study.

K. Marx, "Preface to a Contribution to the Critique of Political Economy." A classic short statement of the basic outline of Marx's theory.

K. Marx and F. Engels, *Manifesto of the Communist Party.*

※ F. Engels, *Socialism: Utopian and Scientific.* Parts I and III of this work contain a useful summary of some main parts of the theory of historical materialism.

F. Engels, *The Origin of the Family, Private Property and the State.* Engels' account of the transition from early tribal communism to class society. It also contains his account of the state and of the origin of the subjugation of women.

V.I. Lenin, *Imperialism, the Highest Stage of Capitalism* (in Vol. 22 of the *Collected Works*).

V.I. Lenin, *What the "Friends of the People" Are and How They Fight the Social Democrats* (in Vol. 1 of the *Collected Works*). An early pamphlet of Lenin's the first part of which contains a useful presentation of the principles of Marxist explanation and classification.

The quote from Engels is in his *Speech at the Graveside of Karl Marx* available in most collections of the writings of Marx and Engels.

Chapter 5

MARXISM AND OTHER THEORIES

In the *Communist Manifesto,* Marx and Engels wrote that all previous history has been the history of class struggle. They meant that the movement and development of history could only be understood by seeing how ruling classes strive to maintain their control of the means of production against the interests of other classes in society. They also meant that these means of production have created the possibility and the necessity for the emergence of new ruling classes. Major changes in history have occurred when a new class organizes itself as a class, succeeds in taking political power away from a previous ruling class and uses this power to consolidate its own domination over production.

The historical materialist insists that in striving to understand people's problems it is necessary first to look at the conditions of life and work they have to contend with in a class-divided society. For example, some people attempt to explain the main problems of farmers by appealing to abstract conflicts, such as "industry versus agriculture" or "urban versus rural life." Marxists look at the effects on farmers of the big urban development corporations, agribusiness and retailers like Loblaws and Dominion, whose *class* interests lead them to spoil the land, squeeze out family farms and monopolize food production and distribution, solely for private profit.

Similarly, the massive cutbacks in higher education across the country are often explained by such statements as: "society overextended itself in the 1960s and now cannot provide jobs for college graduates, so it must cut back on education." Marxists have always been suspicious of explanations that refer to "society" in general. They note instead that through provincial governments the large corporations urged rapid university and college expansion in the 1960s — at the taxpayer's expense. At that time they anticipated a need for more highly skilled workers. Now the same corporations are failing to provide jobs and have created the inflationary situation that leads to cutbacks.

Marxists maintain that unless you examine the class interests and other economic factors behind these problems, you will not root out their causes and organize change. There are several alternatives to this point of view. The most popular ones agree that the movement of history must be understood in terms of struggle, but they deny that economic, class struggle is the most important. A full criticism of each of these theories is not possible in this work, so I will only indicate how historical materialism differs from them in order to better explain the Marxist view.

STRUGGLE OF EVERYONE AGAINST EVERYONE ELSE

One popular non-Marxist view of society contends that there is a constant struggle among a multitude of "interest groups." In political science circles this theory is called the theory of "power politics." Since the 1950s it has become a dominant theory in North American universities and is promoted as an alternative to Marxism. This theory maintains that there are many interest groups, all fighting it out — big business, labour unions, community groups, service organizations, religious groups, social clubs, and so on. History is understood as the changing relations of interest groups as they come into conflict with one another.

On its theoretical side the power politics theory promotes views we have already criticized: it is a version of the theory that everyone is naturally selfish and joins "interest groups" to further selfish ends. On the practical side, this theory does not help one to understand contemporary society. Capitalists control the nature and extent of production in a society. They hire and fire thousands of workers at a time and pour huge amounts of money into political campaigns. It is absurd to consider this powerful force as just one interest group among others, along with some community group or social club. And, despite anti-union propaganda, even the largest trade unions command only a fraction of the wealth held by big corporations.

To the Marxist it is incorrect to see the dominant class in a society as just one interest group among others. A society's dominant or ruling class determines the nature of the society as a whole. It controls the government, determines the major principles around which society is organized (for private profit in our society), and is responsible for the existence and nature of many of the other groups in society. These groups are either organized by a ruling class to serve its ends or are organized by people to combat its bad effects on their lives. Moreover, this theory conveniently forgets the large majority of the population, such as unorganized workers, who are not in any "interest group" at all, but who are nonetheless locked in daily struggle with their bosses.

BIG GUYS VERSUS LITTLE GUYS

Prior to the one-day general strike, or "day of protest," in October, 1976, all the pro-business newspapers carried the expected articles, editorials and interviews denouncing the strike. One theme they pushed hard was that the strike was selfishly planned by "big labour" with no regard for the interests of the unorganized "little guys." This line played on a theory that is widespread in pro-capitalist social science. Fascist movements have also used it to attract people who feel alone and isolated. The theory maintains that the basic struggle in society is between the individual and big, impersonal organizations or bureaucracies.

Pro-business newspapers are quick to drag the theory out against unions but do not fall all over themselves to condemn Stelco, Bell Telephone, the Liberal or Tory political parties and other organizations that obviously do run roughshod over individual working people. Also, while it is true that some trade unions are large, they cannot be compared with the large corporations. Even if unions had the economic strength of corporations, it would be incorrect to see them as equally oppressive, as any worker who can remember the days before many trade unions were built can tell you.

True, under right-wing leadership some unions have pursued narrow and selfish policies, and there is a constant struggle within most unions on the part of rank-and-file members against sell-out union bureaucracy and for greater democracy. The October 14 strike itself was the result of pressure from rank-and-file unionists. Top CLC leadership for the most part resisted the pressure as long as they could. But by and large the trade union movement does *not* set itself against individual working people. Since they know that there is strength in numbers, most trade unions actively attempt to organize the unorganized — the more unorganized workers there are, the lower bosses can pay.

Literature and movies also reflect this theory of big guys versus little guys when they create heroic, but usually doomed individuals who find themselves confronted by a mindless "machine." It doesn't make much difference what the machine is — a corporation, the state or a union.

The grain of truth in the theory is that individuals under capitalism are frustrated by most of the big organizations they come into contact with. Corporations, the government and the civil service have no way of dealing with individual needs and complaints, and in fact do not care about individuals' well-being. Their main concern is promoting private profit and maintaining the *status quo*. Their message is loud and clear: we are all helpless victims of an impersonal machine and nothing we can do will change anything. But to a Marxist, the most foolish thing working people can do is to give up hope or to attempt to fight these organizations alone. People must *unite,* thus becoming strong enough to challenge oppressive forces. And to do this we need very clear and specific ideas about just who these oppressive forces are. It doesn't help much to be told that the enemy is "bigness" in general.

STRUGGLE AMONG LEADERS

Perhaps the most popular bourgeois theory about history, and the one most often taught in Canadian schools, is that it is a series of struggles among individual leaders. When ancient history is taught we read about the intrigues of men like Alexander and Caesar. When contemporary politics is discussed it is in terms of the personalities of politicians. Marxists do not ignore the crucial roles that individuals can play in certain situations. For instance, in a revolutionary situation someone with the leadership skills of Lenin might make a big difference.

However, it would be wrong to conclude from this that the whole of history can be explained by seeing what great individuals are around and what they think and do. In the first place, what needs to be examined are the situations in which people *can* play key roles. Lenin did not create a revolutionary situation in Czarist Russia. This was done by economic oppression, participation of Czarist Russia in World War I, a long history of progressive and revolutionary struggles on the part of the people and many other factors. In the second place, Lenin did not lead the Russian Revolution

52

alone. The workers, peasants and intellectuals who formed the Bolshevik Party led this revolution, even though Lenin certainly played a very important role within that party. An effect of the "great man" approach to history is that it leads people to single out some one individual in a social movement and to ignore the rest.

To see how incorrect this approach is, one needs to look at the realities behind the rise of individual leaders and their decisions. To take one example, Nazism and World War II are often explained as a result of Hitler's ability to dupe the German people. But if you look at the actual history of Germany in the 1930s you find that the rise of Nazism there depended on many economic and political factors — severe economic depression, divisions in the left, the devastation of the war. One important factor was that capitalists, who feared socialist revolution, poured huge sums of money into the Nazi party.

It usually doesn't matter how much bourgeois politicians differ in what they say or what kind of personalities they have. Trudeau was supposed to be the great defender of individual freedom — and a slightly radical person. This image did not keep him from imposing the War Measures Act in 1970, which subjected all Canada to martial law. In 1974 Trudeau won an election over his Tory rival, Stanfield, in a bitter struggle over the policy of "wage and price controls" (better known to working people as simply "wage controls"), where he opposed the controls. As these words are being written, we have wage controls imposed by none other than P.E. Trudeau.

Yet another example of the same sort of thing is the succession of U.S. Presidents who, despite their different parties, different policies and different personalities, all continued to escalate the war in Vietnam until the U.S. was defeated. The truth is that when the capitalists who dominate the Canadian economy find it in their interests to have wage controls and when U.S. ruling circles wanted to pursue the war, it was of secondary importance who happened to be Prime Minister or President at the time.

STRUGGLE OF IDEAS

Another alternate theory is that the struggle of ideas is primary. Advocates of this view point to the fact that in every period of history there have been contesting ideas in philosophy, science, religion and art. Marxism does not underestimate the importance of the battle of ideas in history. In all periods of history there have been bitter struggles between theories favouring progress and revolution and those favouring the *status quo*. Indeed, Marx and Engels saw their own works as a part of this struggle. But the existence of that struggle isn't the issue. The issue is whether the battle of ideas is the fundamental cause of historical change. Marxists ask where these ideas come from that people struggle over. And the historical materialist finds that they come out of a society's economic class structure and struggles.

Marx and Engels looked back over the history of ideas and found that the dominant beliefs of any period — the ideas taught in schools, preached in churches, published in the news — have been those promoted to further the interests of the dominant class. When feudal lords were dominant the leading ideas were that some people (the feudal lords) were born better than other people (like serfs who worked for them), and the best thing people could do was to keep their natural place in life. When capitalists became the dominant class, the leading ideas were that free enterprise, rugged individualism and competition were the natural state of things. Leading ideas under socialism are those promoting cooperation and the dignity of labour.

Because of these facts Marx and Engels criticized pro-socialist "Utopian" theorists of their time. Utopian socialists saw the battle of ideas as primary, which meant that in their political work they limited themselves to fighting for educational reforms and programs to enlighten political leaders. These Utopians thought that if only the leaders of a society could be convinced that their pro-capitalist ideas were wrong, then they would convert the society to socialism. What the Utopians failed to understand was that pro-capitalist ideas are not the cause of capitalism. Rather they are tools used by capitalists to maintain their class position. Of course it is necessary to combat these ideas among working people, thus striving to take away one of the capitalists' tools, but by itself this battle cannot end the capitalist system.

HUMANS VERSUS NATURE

Some environmentalists have recently expressed the view that the primary struggle is with nature. It is argued that whatever differences human may have among themselves, these are not as great as the antagonism between humans and nature. This is especially so, they say, since humans have overpopulated the earth, polluted the air and water, and in general let technology run rampant.

Now, Marxists do not deny that humans have to struggle in

54

the face of nature. In very long-range terms, it might be seen as the primary one, since the use of tools and the division of labour come from the need to stay alive in a hostile physical environment; and long after class struggle has disappeared, the struggle with nature will continue. Engels even remarked that in this conflict humans will ultimately lose, since the sun will not last forever. But the question is whether or not the struggle between humans and nature has been the primary one in written history and especially at the present time.

To see that it is not, one needs to ask: what is responsible for the spoilage of nature and how can it be stopped? To the Marxist, and many current environmentalists, the major source of the waste and destruction of our natural environment has been capitalist greed for profit and the characteristic lack of long-range planning. It is true that using throw-away bottles and driving oversized cars contribute to pollution. But somebody has to *produce* throw-away bottles and oversized cars. Capitalists introduced these commodities into the world, and they continue to profit from them. Moreover, the worst spoilage of nature is industrial pollution, which cannot be compared to the pollution caused by individual consumers. Even though relatively inexpensive techniques are available to recycle industrial waste and filter the smokestacks, industrialists refuse to use them, since this would cut into profits. They continue to pour industrial waste into waterways and poisons into the air of our cities.

For the Marxist it is important to keep one's priorities straight in waging any struggle. Now that large segments of the capitalist world are more or less adequately industrialized and the under-developed world needs to start building its own industry, research teams like the Club of Rome, financed by large corporations and pro-capitalist governments, have begun calling for a world freeze on industrialization. Such sudden respect for the conflict with nature is suspicious.

The theory of historical materialism is essential in guiding an effective battle against the spoilage of nature. In the first place, this theory identifies the main offenders — those who produce for profit. Public opinion should be focused on those people and the government forced to legislate against them. In the second place, such long-range coordinated work will be necessary to *reverse* the effects of 200 years of spoilage that only a socialist organization of society is up to the task.

Some people hold that the primary antagonisms are not between economic classes, but between races, ethnic groups, nations or sexes. The long history of racial oppression and persecution is presented as proof. Similarly, national oppression and wars between nations have a long history, and the special subjugation of women is well known, at least by women. It should be noted that each of these views has a right-wing version. White supremacists often maintain that the key struggle in history has been to keep their race "pure." Supernationalists like the Nazis in Germany or right-wing national chauvinists in the U.S. have believed that the most important force of history has been the drive of their respective nations to fulfill a God-given destiny. And to many male chauvinists the struggle between the "male principle" and "female principle" is central. For instance, Sigmund Freud once wrote that women are a major threat to "civilization," because they are too emotional and lack male rationality.

Racism, national chauvinism and sexism are the attitudes, respectively, that some race, nation or sex is naturally superior or inferior to others. Ethnic discrimination — for example the discrimination of Anglo Canadians against Italian Canadians and others — carries with it an attitude in some respects much like racism.

Marxists have been among the leaders in struggles against these attitudes and their effects on people. But, as in the case of pollution, the question is what is primary for understanding history and what is primary for bringing change. The Marxist view is that these things are supported and to a large extent created by ruling-class needs in class society. Marxists also claim that while changing the class structure of society from capitalism to socialism does not automatically eliminate these things, it is absolutely necessary if they are finally to be completely eliminated from human history.

Racial and ethnic antagonisms. The main problem with the theory that racial and ethnic antagonisms are the key to understanding society is that these antagonisms are not found everywhere through human history. I will discuss racism here, but the same arguments apply in the case of ethnic discrimination. It is a matter of debate among anthropologists and historians when racism first appeared in human history. As a widespread phenomenon it is only found relatively recently with the introduction of the slave trade and colonization. Racism became a prevalent attitude when it served a *class* interest to create antagonism between races. Slave traders and those who owned slaves had to regard slaves as inferior forms of life, in order to justify such human misery. It serves the interests of imperialists to regard the people of the places they pillage as inferior.

Look at places where racism and racial struggle are obvious and ask: Who gains and who loses? In South Africa, where racism is official government policy, the white minority industrialists have become rich thanks to having a large work force of Blacks who must work for starvation wages. Similarly, in the U.S., Blacks, Mexican Americans and Puerto Ricans have been sources of cheap labour for capitalists. Racist attitudes among U.S. white workers have helped big business to keep the labour movement divided and wages down, just as English-Canadian discrimination toward French-Canadian and immigrant workers has here. Who profited from the low pay and terrible working conditions experienced by the Orientals who built the railroads: the average white Canadian worker or CP Rail? We also know that it has been trading companies like Hudson's Bay that profited from the outright theft of native people's land.

Since European countries were the first to become capitalist and to engage in widespread imperialist rampages, it is not surprising that white racism is the most prevalent. But where there are class interests at stake racism is not confined to white people. For example, while people of Japanese descent are subject to racist discrimination in Canada and elsewhere, Japanese capitalism, which was built up by imperialist holdings in China and Korea among other places, encourages ethnic discrimination in Japan against Chinese and Koreans. In some countries of the West Indies, racial tension between Blacks and people of East-Indian origin serves the interests of reactionary leaders, since it keeps people divided.

National antagonisms. The view that the major antagonisms in history have been between nations stems from the fact that throughout written history there have been wars, and most wars take place between nations. History books are often little more than lists of wars. Other historical events, like scientific discoveries, economic changes and artistic developments are related to what wars were going on at the time. Just as we needed to ask whose interests are served by racism, we need to ask whose interests are served by war. And it turns out that ruling-class interests are served by both.

The Roman wars against other peoples were not waged for anything as abstract as promoting the "grandeur of Rome." They were waged so that Roman nobles could gain land, goods and slaves.

57

The wars among European countries of the eighteenth and nineteenth centuries were not initiated by popular demand to uphold "national honour," but were started by the various ruling classes involved in an inter-capitalist fight to secure spheres of economic influence. Some twentieth-century wars have been grabs for markets and some have been capitalist attempts to put down socialism. First was the invasion of the Soviet Union in its early days by England, Germany, France and other countries (even Canada sent a contingent); later was the Korean War, and the most recent has been the war in Vietnam. In all these wars, ruling-class interests have *used* nations and national sentiments to further their own ends, just as they use racism. (There is also a progressive side to national sentiments, which will be discussed in chapter twelve.)

It is instructive to note that under socialism, while there are still nations and often quite strong national sentiments, there are not the same feelings of national antagonism. Vietnam is the best example. Even while they were being bombed in the most thorough and inhuman way by U.S. planes, the Vietnamese did not blame the American people or the American nation. They held the present rulers of the U.S. responsible, because they understood that national antagonisms there were sparked by ruling-class interests.

The "battle of the sexes." Antagonisms between men and women and the attitude of sexism that accompanies them are not an obvious component of the economic class structure of society. This is because these antagonisms are literally too close to home. The special problems of women are often felt by them in their very homes, and the men with whom they live are usually completely unconsious of the fact that they treat women as something like servants. Marxism recognizes the special oppression of women, and in fact Frederick Engels was one of the first authors to attempt a scientific explanation of it.

Engels maintained (and much recent anthropology supports him) that in very early societies, men and women held equal positions. Engels argued that the general subjugation of women came into existence only with class society. In our own society it is not hard to see that the subjugation of women serves the interests of capitalists. For one thing women are paid less than men for the same sorts of work, thus providing a pool of cheap labour for business. For another thing, the vast majority of both those women who have jobs and those who do not, have to do the bulk of the work in the home required for feeding their husbands and raising their chil-

58

dren. They must tend to the present workers and raise the future ones. These are functions that capitalism needs performed and it is convenient and inexpensive (for the capitalists) to force the burden of this work on individual women.

Sexist attitudes are very deep rooted. Marxists are just beginning to advance the work Engels started of understanding them. In my own view, one form sexism takes is the attitude that the only natural way to live is in a male-dominated family where the woman's primary and only role is confined to child bearing and care. Many families today require two wages, so the woman is compelled to work. However, if she also *wants* to work, or otherwise to live in a way that doesn't fit in with her "normal" role, then this is supposed to prove there is something wrong with her. It is this sexist attitude also, in my opinion, that underlies the persecution of homosexuals which has always been typical of conservatives and the right wing.

Male chauvinist attitudes and behaviour do not automatically or immediately disappear with the winning of socialism. Nonetheless, the progress that has been made in combating male chauvinism under socialism so far is impressive. Most present-day socialist countries came out of peasant societies with strongly entrenched backward attitudes toward women. For instance, in the Uzbek Republic, a nation of the USSR, women were still wearing veils at the time of its socialist revolution. But even with very backward attitudes to combat, socialism has made huge advances in the position of women.

While chauvinism in capitalist countries makes it very difficult for women to participate in politics except in rare and exceptional cases, women in socialist countries have increasingly become a significant proportion of the elected leadership in government. In the Soviet Union, for example, more than one third of the deputies to the Supreme Soviet (the body roughly comparable to our Parliament) are women. (In fact, the 1975 chairperson of one of this body's two chambers — the Soviet of Nationalities — was a woman from the Uzbek Republic.) About 70 per cent of Soviet doctors and over 30 per cent of engineers and lawyers are women. In Cuba, where women's participation in government has also grown, there was recently passed a law that a working woman must do no more than 50 per cent of the housework and child care in her home. The other half must be shouldered by her husband.

These, and comparable examples that can be found in all the socialist countries, do not prove that the position of women and male chauvinist attitudes change immediately. But they do show what a crucial difference a change in the class structure of a country has in the struggle of women to gain an equal place in society.

There are further alternatives to the Marxist approach to history and society, and of course there is more that could be said about each of the views discussed above. They have been selected because they are the most popular alternative theories to Marxism. Undoubtedly they are the most popular because they at least are concrete and reflect *some* degree of truth. There *are* national, sexual and other antagonisms. Large institutions in our society *do* run roughshod over individual people. There *are* battles of ideas and conflicts among different interest groups. Marxism does not deny that these things exist. Rather it maintains that they cannot be understood unless seen within the context of the class struggles of a society, and that major progress in combating things like national chauvinism, sexism and so on cannot be made in our society unless working people engage in active class struggle against capitalism and gain socialism.

Chapter 6

THE WORKING CLASS AND THE REVOLUTIONARY PARTY

Socialism will not come into existence automatically. People must organize themselves for the purpose of taking control of the means of production and orienting society to the needs of working people. This reorientation requires that the political power of the state be taken out of the hands of capitalists. The natural questions that arise are *which* people will take the lead in doing these things and *how* will they do it.

THE WORKING CLASS

Various pro-socialists have given different answers to the first question. The Utopian socialists thought that present-day capitalists and political leaders themselves could take the lead if only they would read the right books. Others have seen intellectuals taking the lead, or students. The important role of peasants in earlier revolutions has led some to think of them as the leading force. It has even been suggested that the lumpenproletariat is the key to socialist revolution.

The Marxist view is that the working class, and most importantly, the industrial portion of it, can and will lead revolutionary struggle. The Marxist reasons for this have already been outlined in chapter three, as have some Marxist responses to criticisms of this view. In that chapter it was argued that capitalism itself creates in the working class a force with both the incentive and the means to end the system of capitalism. To this argument I will just add two more considerations.

In the first place, the interests of the working class coincide with those of almost every other group in society. Modern productive forces are controlled by capitalists who cannot use them in a way beneficial to everyone, and what is more they have little desire to do so. The only solution is for the working class itself to take charge of the means of production. Since the working class has no interest in living off the labour of others, this initial act will be decisive for ending the division of society into classes altogether. The proletariat's purpose is to control the conditions and the fruits of its *own* work so that the means of production are used rationally. Almost every other group in society (like farmers, the petty-bourgeoisie and students) an interest in the means of production being rationally employed by the people who actually work, since this would eliminate the main source of problems they confront. The anarchy of capitalist production and the capitalist drive for private profit affect everyone. Because the working class is the largest and strongest class in society that stands opposed to the capitalist class, it is obviously in the interests of other groups to ally with it. At the same time it is in the interests of the working class to join with as many other groups and classes in society as possible, because capitalism is not easily toppled.

Another reason the working class will play the leading role is that its interests go *beyond* those of other groups. At a certain point in the history of a society the contradiction between social work and private ownership becomes intolerable to the working class. At that stage the capitalist class can do nothing to meet working-class demands, and the working class is left with no option but to take over the state and take control of the means of production themselves. This is not the case with other groups in industrial society. Due to their small size or to the special and restricted nature of their demands, it is possible for patchwork measures within the system of capitalism to hold off revolutionary efforts indefinitely. Thus, the working class is more reliably revolutionary than other groups.

It is true that the working class does not always express revolutionary ideas or intentions. For instance, during periods of relative prosperity (such as that purchased by capitalists through imperialism) the working class does not see socialist revolution as in its interests. But a scientific analysis of society looks beyond temporary appearances. If you survey the world today and see who is in the leadership of revolutionary struggles in countries that are very close to socialism, you will see that it is the working class. A study of the history of the Canadian working class will show that it has always included segments that favoured socialism and that these segments are on the increase.

THE REVOLUTIONARY PARTY

Social revolutions do not come about easily. A ruling class does not give up its position willingly, but uses the power of the state to protect it. For a socialist revolution to succeed it is necessary for the working class and its allies to have an organization that can take the power of the state from capitalists and rebuild the state to serve working people's needs. An organization formed for any other purpose will not do, even if it is a working-class organization. A trade union, for example, is geared toward making gains within the capitalist system, not to toppling the system. What the working class needs is its own revolutionary political party. It needs an organization that will gather together the most politically conscious and capable members of the working class and others who see the need for socialist transformation of society (what Marxists call the "vanguard" of the proletariat).

An organization is needed that can bring careful scientific analysis based on Marxist theory to bear on concrete political practice. This organization must combine the ability to make correct decisions about a course of action with the ability to carry them out. For the former such an organization requires democratic decision-making procedures so that political experience and knowledge can be shared and discussed to the fullest. To be effective, the organization must have the resolution to act in a united way once a decision has been made. That is, the organization requires what Marxists call "democratic centralism." The working class needs a political party with these specific features as a weapon against capitalists, who have proven that they will do everything in their power to prevent socialism.

Marx and Engels helped to build one such party, the Communist League. Lenin, of course, was instrumental in building the first revolutionary party to win a socialist revolution. He also wrote a good deal about the need for revolutionary parties and the practical problems involved in building them. Since the time of Marx and Engels working people have formed Communist Parties in nearly every country of the world (the Communist Party of Canada was formed in 1921), and these parties have provided the key leadership in the many movements to gain and construct socialism so far.

In calling working-class revolutionary parties "political" Marxists do not mean that they exist primarily to run socialist candidates in political elections. When the working class is strong enough important gains can be made through elections, but this is not all that a revolutionary party exists to do. They are political in the broader sense that they aim, alone or in coalition with other socialist political organizations, to take state power from capitalism and to reconstruct the state in accord with new relations of production. To achieve this goal a revolutionary party of the working class is needed to link up and coordinate the many struggles working people are engaged in. On the economic front, working people are engaged in fights against different bosses and in different industries. There are community struggles against landlords and around municipal matters. Many workers become involved in national struggles for self-determination and freedom from imperialism. There are battles waged for the rights of those discriminated against because of their race or sex. All these issues need to be coordinated. But to achieve the necessary level of coordination the working class requires a political party that can gain an overview of working people's problems and act in the best long-range interests of everybody who suffers from the effects of the capitalist system.

In addition to forging the broadest possible alliances within a country, a revolutionary working-class party must look beyond its borders to help build international working-class unity — to defend what Marxists call "proletarian internationalism." When working classes that have already achieved socialism find their societies under political, economic or even threatened military attack from capitalist-dominated countries, workers' parties in the capitalist countries must defend socialism. When working people in other countries are striving to free themselves from capitalism or imperialism they require international support from other working people. Vietnam is an example of one place where international support was most important in preventing an imperialist victory. In their efforts to combat Canadian and U.S. imperialism, the people of the Caribbean (among others) now require well-organized Canadian support. Already the socialist working-class movements in Western Europe are coming under increased attack and will need organized working-class support from around the world. Again, to organize this support, a revolutionary party of the working class is needed.

A party is needed to raise revolutionary consciousness, because it is necessary for people to understand the underlying *class* nature of struggles they are engaged in. For instance, in striving to reverse cutbacks in social services such as welfare or child care, it is important to see that these cutbacks are being carried out in the interests of capitalism and can be reversed if the government is forced to tax capitalist profits. In bringing class analyses and subsequent tactics to people's struggles, a revolutionary party helps in winning those struggles and also educates people about the nature of class society and the need to change it. To accomplish this task a party is needed to expose capitalist lies and bring much-needed information about what actually goes on in the world, through its own publications.

The need for a revolutionary political party has been challenged by some who otherwise favour some kind of social change. I will conclude this chapter by listing some alternative approaches.

REFORMISM

One view, called "reformism," is that things will change gradually through greater and greater reforms. Hence, revolutionary struggle is considered unnecessary, and if a working-class party is required at all, it should not be a revolutionary one. Failing to see how the state serves ruling-class interests, reformists suggest that governments as they are constituted under capitalism can be trusted to carry out reforms once public opinion has been mobilized. "Economism" is one version of reformism that Lenin took special pains to combat. Its advocates think that workers' economic — mainly trade union — struggles alone will eventually lead to socialism by forcing more and more economic reforms on the capitalist system.

Full critiques of alternatives to a revolutionary party proposed by otherwise progressively-minded people are not possible in an introductory book. But I will indicate the main lines along which Marxists react to them. Reformists assume that human aspirations can be realized within the present system or else they assume that reform measures will lead gradually and automatically to socialism. Marxists disagree with both these assumptions, and they do not think the capitalist state can be trusted to carry out the most important reforms that working people need.

As long as the major sources of wealth and power in society are privately owned and controlled only minimal reforms can be won or kept. This does not mean that gains like unemployment insurance and universal medical coverage are insignificant. But these reforms do not alter the main anti-working class orientation of the capitalist system. Moreover, all it takes is a threatened cut in profits for capitalists to take back reforms people have won. Reforms can make capitalists cut into profits a little for limited periods of time if they have no other choice. But they can never force them to give up the whole show and allow a reorientation of industry and government to serve working people's needs. At some point people have to organize to take the means of production away from the capitalists. It is to be hoped that working people will be so well organized and determined that this can be done peacefully, thus preventing the capitalists from protecting their interests through violence. But however socialism comes about, it will have to be very deliberately carried out with full knowledge of the powerful opposition to socialism on the part of capitalists.

ANARCHISM

Anarchists hold that revolutionary parties of the kind Marx and Engels had in mind would be elitist, authoritarian institutions which would stifle revolution. Many anarchists confine themselves to criticizing Marxists. Others propose that revolutions should be the product of many relatively small collectives, each striving for worker or community control in its own area of work or residence.

While the underlying assumption of reformism is that social transformations will take place automatically, anarchists assume that transformations will take place spontaneously. To Marxists it would be a most astonishing accident if scattered collectives of people not only took control of their factories or communities, but also carried out a social revolution. Surely their various efforts would have to be coordinated and given common direction. How can this be done without a disciplined political party? Anarchists give different answers to this question, but, Marxists claim, all their plans either do not allow for enough coordination and discipline to be effective, or they introduce the concept of a revolutionary party under a different name.

SOCIAL DEMOCRACY

Social democracy is an approach that does not deny the need for a political party, but denies that it should be *revolutionary*. Along with reformists social democrats share the view that socialism (though many social democrats do not like to use this word) will *evolve* by gradual reforms. But unlike other reformists, they think there should be a political party to lead this evolution. Marxists also challenge the assumption of social democracy that the government is neutral. Social-democratic political parties typically confine themselves to electoral work. Their aim is to gain a larger and larger voice in basically pro-capitalist governments and thereby effect reforms without rocking the boat and being labelled "revolutionaries."

This strategy overlooks the fact that there are limits beyond which capitalists are not prepared to go. Moreover, capitalists do not have to allow certain reforms, since they have a great deal of control over who is elected to public office and what decisions are made by governments. They also have ways of getting around governmental measures if they don't like them, and they are prepared to work outside the government if they have to. When the pro-capitalist Liberal Party formed a government in 1974 with a clear popular mandate to oppose wage controls, that did not stop it from introducing those very controls.

As for the "keep respectable" strategy, anybody who confines himself to pressing only for demands considered respectable within a capitalist-controlled government (and with a capitalist-controlled press) will never be able to advance demands that seriously challenge the capitalist system.

Anarchists and others charge that the Marxist theory leads to an elitist party standing above the working class and to anti-democratic organizations. By this charge they mean that inside the party democracy is sacrificed to centralism and that after socialism has been achieved the party acts in an anti-democratic way toward the people. Social democrats and other reformists often add that a revolutionary party runs the risk of being discredited, harassed and made illegal by the state.

The criticism about elitism comes from confusion about the theory as well as the practice of revolutionary parties. It was the view of Marx and Engels that these parties grow *out of* the working class. They are made up of working-class people and their allies from other classes whose experience in people's organizations (such as trade unions, the women's movement, and so on) has taught them the need for such a party. Sometimes this is said to be contradicted by the fact that the best-known theoreticians and spokesmen for revolutionary political parties have not themselves been from

67

working-class origins. This is true. Marx, Engels, Lenin and Castro are examples; however, there have always been working-class revolutionary leaders as well. In the early days of working-class revolutionary organization it would have been surprising if some important leaders were not from other classes, since these were the people who were able to acquire the education necessary to research and develop the theories of revolutionary struggle. Moreover, Marx, Engels, Lenin and others were participants in much larger movements, so it is an example of the "great man" theory of history to think of their parties as mere extensions of a few personalities.

Are anti-democratic tendencies possible in revolutionary political parties? Of course they are. Any time an organization with chains of command, committee structures and so on is formed there will be the possibility that the democratic side of "democratic centralism" will become weakened. The serious problems and the pressures that confront a revolutionary party in the early stages of socialism make possible policies that work against democracy as well as ones that work for it. Are there dangers of police harassment? Of course. Any party in a capitalist society that openly works for an end to capitalism will be subject to harassment of various forms.

But if the Marxist theory is correct that capitalism must go and that a revolutionary party of the working class is necessary to win socialism, then there seem to be just two alternatives. One is to sit on the sidelines and moan about real and imagined problems and dangers. The other is to join the struggle and work to solve the problems and confront the dangers.

READINGS FOR CHAPTER SIX

K. Marx & F. Engels, *Manifesto of the Communist Party,* Parts II, III, IV.

F. Engels, *On the History of the Communist League.*

V.I. Lenin, *Left Wing Communism: An Infantile Disorder (Collected Works,* Vol. 31). A treatment of parliamentary and extra-parliamentary roles of a revolutionary party.

Chapter 7

WORKING-CLASS CONSCIOUSNESS

In chapter four I suggested that in determining what economic class a person belongs to, Marxists are interested in what role that person actually plays in production, not in what the person happens at some time to *think* his or her class position is. But this does not mean that Marxists are indifferent to what working people think about their own economic class position. Quite the contrary. Marx, Engels and Lenin knew that a successful revolution was not possible unless working people acquired class consciousness. This does not just mean that working people must come to think of themselves as workers rather than bosses — workers know they are not bosses. Nor does it just mean that a class-conscious worker is one who sees his or her boss as an enemy, out to get as much work for as little pay as possible. Again, most workers are well aware of this.

Very little Marxist literature is written specifically about class consciousness. However, Lenin wrote some important pamphlets on the subject, and Antonio Gramsci, one of the founders of the Italian Communist Party, wrote extensively about consciousness while imprisoned in Mussolini's jails. The work of these two men, and scattered comments by other Marxists, suggest that two elements are required for full revolutionary class consciousness.

First, a worker must understand the need to get rid of the entire *system* of capitalism, rather than just to combat some of its worst effects. Second, working people must recognize the possibility of doing this task *themselves* by organizing as a class against capitalism, leading other segments of the population in a successful revolution and constructing a pro-working class state to replace the pro-capitalist one. Put more briefly, full class consciousness requires identifying the system of capitalism as the main enemy and being prepared to take a leadership role in changing society.

Capitalism maintains its rule not just by the use or threatened use of police force. It also maintains its rule by creating a situation where working people are *confused* about the class nature of society, *divided* from one another and *without confidence* in their own ability to lead.

CONFUSION AND DIVISION

Life itself under capitalism promotes confusion and divisions among people. Our educational system is well-known for its inadequacy, and our days and weeks are divided up in such a way that it is hard to find the time to reflect on the nature of society. At the work place workers are divided between skilled and unskilled workers and by various forms of discrimination in pay. In society they are divided between the employed and the unemployed; and since in our cities people are removed from their neighbours, people are divided by where they live. Marxist sociologists and psychologists are just beginning to study these things.

However, the sources of confusion and division I will briefly discuss are mainly *ideological* in nature, that is, they affect people's ideas about themselves and about society as a whole.

On the one hand, there is an overriding attempt by the "idea" machinery to discourage serious political thought of any kind among working people. On the other hand, there are some myths quite deliberately promoted in bourgeois propaganda. Three of the most important are: that capitalism is good, that socialism is evil and that you can trust the state. There are also many attitudes that serve to divide and confuse people. I will discuss: "me-firstism," certain effects of religion, racism (and ethnic and national chauvinism), sexism and anti-intellectualism.

De-politicization. "De-politicization" is the attempt to stop working people from thinking about and discussing important political ideas. Capitalists prefer to have people worrying only about their personal short-range problems or escaping from their cares by getting drunk or watching mind-rot on television. This is why serious political questions (like: Why not socialism?) occupy very little air time or page space on T.V. or in popular magazines, and why politically-minded people who do raise such issues are pictured as fanatics. Politics is promoted as the kind of cloakroom scheming and

70

election-time promise-making that bourgeois politicians engage in, rather than as reflecting on our society and organizing to change it.

The de-politicized worker is one who views himself or herself as alone, isolated from other working people. Capitalists prefer to have working people think this way. They do not want workers, or anybody else who is subject to the oppression of their profit system, to recognize that they share this situation with many others and have the ability to change it by taking united action. This is why it is made very difficult for working people in one part of the country (or even of a province or a city) to find out the conditions of life and work of those in another part, much less to find out what organized action is taken by others. This is also why capitalism tries to rob people of their own histories.

We all know that, even though imperfect, things like workers' compensation for injuries on the job exist today. But how many know the history of hard campaigns waged by working people's movements that finally forced this and other benefits through? Despite occasional lip-service to the "multi-cultural" character of Canada, we are taught that it was almost exclusively people of British or French stock who built up the country; though we are not taught the actual history of *working* people from these groups and their struggles. People of other backgrounds (Ukrainian, Chinese, Finnish, Jewish, Japanese, Blacks, and many more) do not learn of the vital roles their forebears played in building Canada or of their heroism in organizing against racial, ethnic and class oppression.

For over a decade students and other groups mobilized against the war in Vietnam and the Canadian government's despicable role in that war as an arms merchant and diplomatic lackey for the U.S. Yet today, only a few years later, college and high school students know practically nothing about the war or about the ways students and other groups organized against it. How could they, when these things are either not presented to them at all or are grossly distorted in schools and the media?

De-politicization can be fought by making people aware of the fact that they are not alone and by helping them to regain the histories of their own struggles. It can be fought also in practice by linking up specific issues people are involved in (with their landlords, in their unions, in attempts to lower prices or to resist discrimination) with broader political issues. In the first place a person must understand the need to organize with others. This is an uphill battle, since de-politicization keeps many from becoming involved in any kind of struggle or confrontation to begin with. On the other hand, it can be surprisingly easy. For example, an individual may initially be concerned only with the landlord's unwillingness to fix the plumbing. A few discussions with other tenants may lead to that same person helping to organize a tenants' association, and the connection between a simple individual complaint and the need for political organization has been made.

The "goodness" of capitalism. I do not think we need to be detained very long with this myth. It had more weight when North-American capitalism was able to deliver some of the goods, that is, to keep wages up and unemployment down in key segments of the work force. Although we still hear regular stories about how the system of "private enterprise" is the best in the world and how anybody can make it to the top, this myth requires that people be too ignorant of what is going on around them. In Canada today inflation and unemployment are both on the rise. The cost of housing is growing almost out of people's reach, and even entertainment is too expensive for many. How can someone reach the top when it's hard to find any job at all?

Even those segments of the Canadian work force that have been highly paid, relative to others or in comparison with workers in other parts of the world, are coming to realize that their position is quite insecure. It was the strength of the large monopolies, resting to a large extent on their imperialist activities, that made possible the famous prosperity in North America. But now the monopolies are in trouble. They are losing more and more of their imperialist holdings and are coming under fire from increasingly large parts of the population.

The result is that they are no longer able to deliver. Canadian workers particularly feel the squeeze. Because most of the monopolies are U.S. based, they cut down on production in Canadian branch plants in response to problems in the U.S.

The "evils" of socialism. In every major newspaper in Canada there are daily articles telling us how undemocratic some socialist country is supposed to be or how many social problems it is supposed to have. This propaganda started with the first successful socialist revolution in 1917 and has been increasing ever since. The propaganda has become more refined since then (it used to be alleged that "Bolsheviks eat babies"), but the basic message has been the same in the papers, on T.V., in popular literature and in schools — everywhere that people's ideas can be affected. The cumulative effect is to make anti-socialism an automatic and almost unconscious response among Canadian working people. The aim is to produce a frying pan-fire attitude. No matter how bad capitalism is, we are told, socialism is at least as bad, so don't try to change things. Promoting this attitude is a very important part of the capitalist drive to prevent class consciousness. People are much less likely to want to make drastic changes if they think the only alternative is as bad or worse. Instead they will probably adopt an attitude of despair and try to make the best of a bad situation.

Anti-socialist propaganda used to be primarily economic. It was claimed that socialism could not work. By and large this line has now been abandoned. Not only did the predictions of economic collapse prove to be false, but despite all efforts of capitalist powers to prevent it, socialist countries have been growing economically stronger and stronger. Capitalist propaganda cannot completely hide the fact that socialist countries have proven capable of eliminating unemployment, of providing adequate old age security, free education at all levels, inexpensive housing and free medical treatment, as well as having become major world industrial powers. And as these countries continue to increase production of consumer items, the charge that luxury items are scarce in socialist countries is being heard less frequently.

The main claim of anti-socialists today is that socialist countries are undemocratic. Since I will go into this question in chapter nine, I will not discuss it here except to mention that this charge hinges partly on lying and partly on isolating the worst anti-democratic measures and mistakes made during certain periods of socialist growth. Claiming that these errors and problems prove that socialism is always and everywhere anti-democratic, anti-socialist propaganda completely ignores the essentially democratic nature of socialism.

Socialists in Canada respond to anti-socialist propaganda in various ways. Some *agree* with it and claim that the socialist world, or some segment of it, isn't really socialist. Often the Soviet Union — the oldest and strongest socialist country — is singled out by these people. This attitude plays into the hands of the bourgeoisie. Most working people interpret this as an admission that the press is right and that the people of the USSR went through the difficulties of revolution for nothing. (I have observed that socialists who disown the socialist world generally rely exclusively on "facts" reported by the pro-capitalist press. I have also noted that it seems much easier to be a socialist and to be accepted in non-socialist circles if one is quick to point out that he or she opposes present-day actual socialism or at least the socialism in the Soviet Union.)

In my opinion, the correct response is, first, to attempt to bring facts about the basic democratic character of present-day socialism to working people's attention. Marxists should at least encourage people to gain a broader view by reading material from socialist countries that gives their side of the case. Second, it is necessary to have realistic views about socialism. Present-day, existing socialism is a complex historical phenomenon. Its weaknesses, as well as its strengths, need to be understood by examining the concrete conditions of its development in different countries. Such a realistic viewpoint is important not only for understanding present-day socialism, but also to shift Canadian working people's major focus of attention (where capitalists do not want it) to the concrete conditions and possibilities of gaining socialism and building it with the fewest problems *in Canada.*

The trustworthiness of the government. The third myth I want to mention is the one that says even if capitalists are opposed to the interests of working people, we still have an impartial governmental system that will protect our interests when big business gets too rough. This myth is especially prevalent around election time, when the spokesmen of the parties of big business make pious claims to speak for all the people, and the press is full of stories about how democratic Canada is. Since the next chapter is devoted to the Marxist analysis of the state, discussion of this myth can be set aside for now. As working people learn first-hand whose interests the government serves, this bit of propaganda is becoming harder to peddle. The recent wave of government cutbacks, both federally and provincially in education and health services, coupled with government strike-breaking and stronger anti-labour legislation, speak louder than election-time words about government impartiality.

Me-firstism. Me-firstism is an attitude quite easily spread around in a capitalist society, since the capitalists believe and act on it themselves. It relates to the view discussed in chapter two that everyone is selfish and that people get ahead by being stronger and smarter than everyone else. In addition to providing the major theme of much of our "entertainment," this attitude comes from life and work under capitalism. Capitalist societies are based on competition. Capitalists compete for profits, and workers must compete for jobs. It is not hard to see how some people think that this is how it must always be. This attitude is quite consciously pushed in the bourgeois press, especially when it comes to the unemployed. Unemployed people are pictured as lazy or incompetent sponges on society who have only themselves to blame for being jobless. In fact, unemployed people are part of the working class. They are workers for whom capitalism does not provide jobs. At least it does not provide jobs suitable for people's abilities, and it does not provide the abilities, through education, necessary for what jobs are available.

Me-firstism stands in the way of class consciousness because it leads working people to attribute the success of big businessmen to their intelligence or courage. And it leads working people to blame themselves for their failure to get ahead. Class consciousness is not possible unless people see that capitalists are "ahead" because of other people's work. If people blame themselves for having poor jobs or for being unemployed, they are not going to blame the system and organize to change it.

Religion and class consciousness. Contrary to what some religious leaders say, it is possible for a person to be religious and class conscious. In countries like Italy, many religious people are active Communists. In Poland and other socialist countries there are religious socialists in public office. In Canada many church leaders have been active in the peace movement and in demands for social justice. Some of these people have put the blame for war and injustice where it belongs, on the large corporations and the pro-capitalist governments that serve them. Up to a point a person can even be religious and agree with the theory of Marxism. (However, these people could not interpret religious texts like the Bible literally, since they give a view of history incompatible with historical materialism. Nor could religious people agree with certain philosophical views of Marxism, such as atheism.) To a certain extent religion can *contribute* to class consciousness, since some moral values of religion — the values that preach cooperation and an end to injustice — call attention to the immorality of capitalism. However, religion also works against full revolutionary class consciousness.

I believe there are several reasons for this. One is that being religious tends to make a person more subject to official church doctrines, which are often anti-socialist and pro-capitalist. In fact, the larger churches are themselves part of the capitalist structure, with large land holdings and investments in capitalist enterprises. Another reason is that in some religions, such as Christianity, there is a theory of human depravity, which blames the devil or original sin for human problems. A third reason is that religious belief makes people more susceptible to anti-socialist propaganda. This is partly because the propaganda often has church authority behind it and partly because a recurrent theme of bourgeois propaganda is that socialist countries persecute religion. (In fact religious institutions continue to exist in socialist countries, though due to a real division of church and state they do not hold state-supported positions of economic and political power as in capitalist countries.)

Beginning in the 1960s large numbers of young people began expressing discontent with the crass materialism and injustices of North-American society. Many of these people became involved with the mystical or fundamentalist religious organizations that sprang up everywhere. These organizations are explicitly anti-socialist, and some are funded by certain right-wing business interests from the U.S. and elsewhere. In my opinion, religious organizations like these were able to attract people because they seemed to offer a purpose in life lacking in our society. In fact there *is* a purpose to the way people's daily lives are organized, but it is a purpose not determined by the people themselves. This purpose is to extract as much super-profit as possible for a few capitalists.

A meaningful life for Canadians would be one where we controlled the country ourselves and worked together to build a happy future for ourselves and our children. But such a society will never be built unless working people come to class consciousness, and people will not come to class consciousness if they turn their backs on the material world and look to an afterlife.

Racism, ethnic and national chauvinism. Although there are some important differences among these three attitudes, they can be treated together in this chapter since they have similar effects on people's class consciousness. Canada was founded on racism and chauvinism. Native people welcomed Europeans here in exchange for which their land was stolen from them and a near-genocidal campaign was launched (and is still going on) under cover of racism. In Confederation French Canada was deliberately subjected to English-Canadian rule, and French-speaking Canadians have always been the subject of chauvinistic abuse and exploitation. As each new group of immigrants arrived in Canada, they in turn were subjected to discrimination.

Discrimination affects class consciousness by making other working people the scapegoats for the economic problems created by capitalism. In 1975 Canada was experiencing a sharp increase in unemployment along with a housing shortage and other problems. At this time the government saw fit to release a draft of a policy on immigration which blamed immigrants for unemployment and urban overpopulation. At the same time the large newspapers began to publish unfounded stories linking immigrants to crime. The truth is that Canada is underpopulated and underdeveloped relative to its size and resources. But keeping Canada underdeveloped is in the economic interests of those Canadian capitalists who profit from selling the country out to U.S.-based monopolies. When these policies create unemployment and crowded cities, capitalists are anxious that they not be seen as the cause.

Socialist revolutions are not carried out by angels but by human beings who have grown up in capitalist society with all its distorted values. If working people could become perfect under capitalism, then one of the main reasons for socialism would vanish. After all, socialism is not something to strive for only for economic reasons, but it is necessary in order to raise everybody with truly humanistic values. Nonetheless, attitudes of racism and chauvinism (also the sexist attitudes I shall discuss next) stand in the way of gaining socialism in the first place. These attitudes *dehumanize* people. They lead them to think of large numbers of other people as subnormal. Class consciousness requires that people join in struggle with others to fight the capitalist system and to build a new society. This cannot be done unless people begin to see each other as equals.

Sexism. We have already noted how discrimination against women is very beneficial to capitalists. But is it beneficial to male workers as well? At first glance it might seem to be. Whether his wife works or not, the man does not usually have to do most of the housework, and he may vent his frustrations on his wife. Even if he takes some responsibility for caring for his children, most of the day-to-day work of child care is done by his wife, who also must consider the children's psychological development — how to bring them up as happy, well-adjusted people in a distorted society.

These male benefits are illusory and the sexist attitudes that accompany the oppression of women stand in the way of class consciousness. In the first place, as women's participation in the work force increases in Canada, their lack of trade union protection makes them both vulnerable to increased exploitation and able to be used by capitalists as a way of keeping all wages down. Hence, women's low wages both affect the family income and endanger the male workers' position of strength vis-à-vis the bosses. So it is in the male worker's interests to ally himself with his female co-workers in their struggles against the capitalists. Thus more and more unions in Canada are taking up the demand to end wage discrimination against women, and women are becoming more involved in union affairs and leadership. Sexist attitudes can only inhibit working-class unity.

In the second place, the system of child care and housework favoured by capitalists, where the responsibility for these things falls upon the individual family, has severe disadvantages for the male worker. He is responsible not just for his own well-being, but also for that of his wife and children. This puts quite a bit of pressure on him. It is one thing to quit a bad job or to risk a job by agitating against the bosses if he is responsible only for himself. But when a family depends on his having a regular income, it is quite another matter. Men must join women in fighting for such reforms as government-funded, high quality day care. But they will not do this if they share the sexist attitude that their wives' natural place is at home with the children.

Sexism has certain effects on the male worker's personality that stand in the way of class consciousness. Like racism, sexism is dehumanizing. It leads one to regard 51 per cent of the human population as inferior. Surely it is psychologically healthier for men to join women in fighting their oppression than to contribute to it in their own homes and at their places of work.

Finally, sexism is part and parcel of a whole male-chauvinist psychology that feeds me-firstism. One feature of a male chauvinist society is that women are thought of as having characteristics inappropriate for men. Women show emotion and are encouraged to exhibit humanistic qualities such as kindness and cooperativeness. Men, on the other hand, are supposed to be rugged, emotionless and individualistic. This attitude of rugged manliness leads men to blame themselves for not succeeding. A real man is supposed to be a good provider, who will make lots of money and get ahead because of his individual strength, intelligence and ruthlessness. A man who believes this philosophy is more likely to blame himself for not being enough of a "man" than to blame the system for the failures in his life.

Anti-intellectualism. To reach full class consciousness a person must figure out many things. It is necessary to understand that the main struggle in our society is the class struggle. It is necessary to see through bourgeois propaganda. And, what is perhaps the most difficult, it is necessary to detect in oneself attitudes like racism, national chauvinism and sexism and to understand their bad effects. To do all this people must be able to think rationally and scientifically about their society and themselves. Anti-intellectualism is the attitude that there is something *wrong* with rational, scientific thought. It is giving in to blind prejudice, the attitude: "I may not think much, but I know what I like."

In the eighteenth century emerging capitalism itself was a main force for promoting scientific thinking — especially among professional scientists whose discoveries led to more efficient techniques and machinery and therefore to greater profits. Then as now capitalism has needed science and hence a certain number of people who are capable of scientific thought. But this poses a problem for capitalists, because effective scientific thinking applied to society and history leads to a recognition that their class must go. One capitalist reaction to this problem is to maintain a system that makes it difficult to think about society, especially on the part of working people. This is done in several ways.

People are not born with the ability to think scientifically. They have to be trained. But under capitalism it is not easy to acquire this training. Primary and secondary education in working-class schools is poor (and getting worse, due to cutbacks). It is economically difficult or impossible for the children of workers to go to college. Even in middle-class schools and in colleges people in the social sciences are not trained to think scientifically. Thinking scientifically means striving to understand *why* things are the way they are. This requires developing the critical habits of thought necessary to weigh different theories against the facts and test them for logical coherence. Yet even natural science courses in Canadian schools are mainly a question of just memorizing.

Effective, scientific thinking requires gaining an overview of things by relating different subject matters. Instead, the different disciplines — natural sciences, social sciences and cultural subjects — are so narrowly specialized that connections are hard to make. Scientific thinking is critical thinking. It is thinking that does not accept anything on faith, but that strives to get to the truth even if this means challenging accepted views. Students are not encouraged to think critically but to accept the Establishment theories of their teachers, especially in the study of politics and history. Putting all these things together, it is not hard to understand why someone who has been denied the ability to think in a scientific way would take the anti-intellectual attitude: Who needs it anyway?

Another way that anti-intellectualism is spread is by having people associate intelligence with typical Establishment "intellectuals," such as most of those who teach social science or humanities courses in universities, write books on politics or culture, and are interviewed on T.V. These people are often snobs, experts at putting other people down, and are deliberately obscure when they talk or write. When you can understand them, they usually have nothing to say to the needs of working people. If thinking scientifically means being like them, then who would want to be scientific?

In fact, Establishment "intellectuals" are themselves among the worst anti-intellectuals. Pro-capitalist "intellectuals" today spend most of their time promoting scepticism — doubt — about the possibility and desirability of rational, scientific thought. I will discuss scepticism further in chapter eleven.

Thirdly, anti-intellectualism is practically worshipped through *irrationality* in entertainment. In popular music, for example, feeling and thinking are set in opposition to one another, as if a person had to choose between having deep feelings or understanding things. In the movies, the typical hero is someone who violently and thoughtlessly acts on gut emotions. Under the guise of "spontaneity," mindlessness has become a virtue.

Now, more than ever, revolutionary struggle needs to be guided by carefully pursued scientific study. To some extent this is made possible by some middle-class intellectuals joining the working-class struggle and putting their skills at its disposal. Marx, Engels and Lenin were such people. But it is equally important for workers to acquire the abilities of scientific thinking themselves, which is made difficult in an atmosphere of widespread anti-intellectualism.

LEADERSHIP CONFIDENCE

Recognizing the class nature of society and the need to eliminate capitalism as a social system is not enough for revolutionary working-class consciousness. It is also necessary for the working class of a country to gain the confidence to lead such a struggle. All the factors mentioned above that confuse and divide people also work against their reaching this recognition. However, this aspect of class consciousness is not just, or primarily, a matter of overcoming

80

bourgeois propaganda, but of gaining practical experience in leadership.

Reform action. One important way that revolutionary confidence is built is through reform activity, such as trade union activity. Any time working people are able to organize and force capitalism to make even a small concession they gain confidence in their ability to take the initiative against capitalism. It is for this reason that Marxists reject the position they call "ultra-leftist" — that all reform movements "support the system" and work against revolution.

At the same time, however, Marxists also caution against the reformist view that reform activity is enough to solve the problems in society. At a certain point it is necessary for the working class and its allies to change the social system altogether. As mentioned in chapter six Lenin criticized the version of reformism, called economism, which held that trade unionism was the only kind of organized activity the working class needed. The limitations of this perspective will be taken up again in chapter twelve when I return to the topic of "reform and revolution." One of its effects is to dampen revolutionary working-class consciousness. It leads working people to believe that the only kinds of gains they are able to make within a capitalist system are limited gains for economic reform. Although most economistic reformists do not intend it, the attitude thus plays into the hands of right-wing trade union leaders whose approach is that workers should leave the struggle to them while they compromise with capitalists to win limited advantages. Lenin pointed out that the working class needs to organize politically against the capitalist class.

Working-class political organization. This topic brings us back to the subject of chapter six — the working class' need for its own revolutionary political party. The existence of such a party helps to build working-class consciousness in more ways than just by combating bourgeois propaganda. A revolutionary workers' party provides a concrete organizational framework for the leadership of revolutionary struggle. Without such a framework, socialist revolution can never be more than a good idea. But, as anybody knows, it takes more than good ideas to achieve anything, especially something as difficult as a social revolution.

Another way that a revolutionary workers' political organization builds working-class confidence in its own ability to govern is by *actually governing.* In some capitalist countries Communist Parties, alone or in coalition with other pro-socialist parties, already control some cities and even larger political districts. The record of these parties in such areas is impressive. Fighting against vicious anti-communist propaganda to win elections at first, they usually have little trouble holding their gains in future elections. This is because, unlike pro-capitalist political parties, they offer good leadership. They are more efficient, and they really do put the needs of working people first.

In the process of defeating imperialism through struggles for national self-determination, the workers and peasants in alliance with other classes have been able to form anti-imperialist govern-ments in some developing countries. These societies are not yet socialist ones because not all the major means of production are socially owned and controlled. Also, some pro-capitalist forces (and in some cases even pro-feudal ones) still have influence in the state. However, these societies offer another example of where the work-ing class can learn to govern by actually governing.

A similar situation exists in more industrialized nations, where there is the possibility of forming anti-monopoly govern-ments. The success of the working class in leading the political battles for such governments greatly weakens the economic and political power of the monopolies, and it builds the working class' confidence in its ability to lead.

Working-class leadership. It is doubtful that the working class could gain or hold power without the support of other social groups and classes whose interests are at odds with capitalism. Most previous socialist revolutions have required an alliance of the working class with the majority of the peasantry. Revolution in industrial parts of the world requires alliances of the working class with key segments of the middle classes and with the petty bourgeoisie. It requires that popular discontent for a variety of reasons be brought together in an anti-monopoly alliance. Therefore it is important for the working class not to isolate itself from other sectors of the population and narrowly confine itself to demands that affect only wages and work-ing conditions. It must take up all those issues that hostile pro-capitalist forces confront people with.

In Canada there have been some encouraging signs of this possibility, as parts of the labour movement have taken up stances in support of movements for women's equality, for peace, against racial and ethnic discrimination, for protection of the environment and other popular movements. The working class must not only participate in these struggles, it must also play a leading role in them. This involvement helps ensure the success of those movements, and it inspires confidence in the working class among members of other groups and classes. Above all, it causes members of the working class to realize that they are capable of taking the lead in the transformation of society.

READINGS FOR CHAPTER SEVEN

V.I. Lenin, *What Is to Be Done?* (In Vol. 5 of the *Collected Works).* A critique of reformist, and especially economistic, approaches to working-class organization and of anti-intellectualism.

Antonio Gramsci, *The Modern Prince,* in *Selections from the Prison Notebooks* (New York, New World Paperbacks, 1971, reprinted 1976). In *The Modern Prince,* as in other selections from the *Notebooks,* Gramsci discusses the problem of "hegemony" — roughly, the way a class exercises its control of society by other than violent means — in a way that relates to class consciousness.

Chapter 8

THE STATE

For Marxists the essential point about the state is that it is not above or outside of class struggle. A state exists to serve the interests of a society's dominant class. The state is that part of the superstructure of society that is made up of (1) *enforcement bodies:* courts of law, prisons, police forces and the army; (2) *the government:* including such things as the civil service and legislative bodies like parliaments or city councils; and (3) *government-run services* like the school system.

This definition of the state differs from the one usually given in capitalist society, where it is limited to the government. This pro-capitalist definition conveniently leaves out such things as the army and police, thus masking the coercive function of the state. (Engels once described the state as primarily "bodies of armed men, courts of law and prisons.") The Marxist definition also differs from the view held by some socialists who identify the state with *all* the institutions and ideas that support the rule of a dominant class. This definition is far too broad to be useful. For instance, it does not distinguish among different methods of capitalist domination, and it blurs the difference between conscious support of their system by capitalists and unconscious support by other people.

In the Middle Ages the feudal state apparatus helped kings and lords live relatively well, thanks to the labour of those who did the farming, kept the herds and fought in the wars. The state was also an instrument of class rule in an earlier period when the armies and tax collectors of large empires, like the Roman Empire, enabled a few to get rich. In the Marxist view the state is no more neutral under capitalism than under these previous social-economic systems.

In maintaining a society of private property where there is a sharp division between rich and poor, the capitalists need police forces to guard their property. They need the police also to act as strikebreakers and to thwart working people's attempts to organize themselves. Capitalists need armies to carry on their imperialist activities, to try destroying socialist societies and national-liberation movements, and they even need them to use against people of their own countries to prevent socialism if it becomes necessary. The capitalist state taxes working people to pay for state-run services like the post office and the school system, because capitalists need these things but do not want to pay for them themselves. The state under capitalism runs schools to educate people just enough to be useful employees, but not enough to figure out what is going on in society.

In advanced capitalism, the state runs some industries, again at the taxpayer's expense, when those industries are needed by capitalists, but are unprofitable for the ruling class to run. The state administers research and regulates the economy to a certain extent, not to make a better life for ordinary people, but to promote private profits for the large monopolies. In Canada the very structure of the state helps capitalism. The division of authority between provincial and federal governments is just right for helping large corporations, like the oil industry in the west; but when it comes to local control of funds for things beneficial to working people, it is quite another matter. Anyone who has tried to acquire funds for socially beneficial projects knows how effectively federal, provincial and local levels of government evade the issue by passing the buck back and forth.

Many people find it difficult to understand the class nature of the state. When the police strikebreak it is seen as a result of "police mentality." When the courts pass anti-labour legislation or turn a blind eye to the illegal operations of corporations, it is explained as an effect of the personalities and biases of judges. What this attitude overlooks is that someone has to decide what kinds of police to hire, how to train them and what orders to give them. Judges need to be appointed and supported in the decisions they make. I believe that there are two main reasons why it is sometimes difficult to see how the state under present-day capitalism serves capitalist interests.

For reasons to be presented in the next chapter, the state form favoured by capitalism is "parliamentary democracy." This state form differs from earlier ones in that it is *legally* possible for almost anyone to become a government official, and these officials are supposed to be responsible to the entire voting population of a country. All this is explained to us as proof of how democratic our state is and how it does not serve "special interests." What is more, because of this form of state it is sometimes possible for people who really do have working-class interests at heart to be elected to parliament, and working-class pressure has forced some democratic legislation to be passed.

However, one needs to take a broader view of the state. In the first place if you compare the amount of democratic legislation, which favours working-class interests, with the anti-democratic, pro-big business legislation it is immediately obvious that the first is a drop in the bucket. Moreover, the democratic legislation that is passed, important though it might be for the short-term goals of working people, is almost never of the kind that seriously challenges the system of capitalism. A look at the class background of government leaders in any capitalist country (and Canada is no exception) will show that almost all come from the middle and upper classes and have direct or indirect links with big business. Finally, it is not enough to look at what state officials say and at what legislation they pass, but one must look at what they *do* and at what legislation is *enforced*.

A second reason why it is sometimes difficult to understand the class nature of the capitalist state today has to do with its size and power. In the early days of capitalism, capitalists were famous for wanting to limit the power of the state. However, today the state in industrialized capitalist countries is quite large with many legal controls over the economy and with direct control of some industries. For some people such far-reaching government control is not compatible with capitalism. In fact some equate "big government" with socialism and think that states in advanced capitalist countries today are socialistic. Now it is true that government regulation works against the interests of some capitalists, specifically the smaller capitalist enterprises. However, the large monopolies *profit* from extensive state intervention in the economy, and it is the large monopolies that are the main capitalist forces in the world today.

We live in an era of what Marxists call "state-monopoly capitalism," where a few giant monopolies make extensive use of the state to promote their interests over those of the working class and of other classes in society as well, including small and middle business. It is the large monopolies that support the major pro-capitalist political parties. These monopolies need the state to create markets for their goods, to run segments of the economy at the expense of taxpayers, to supply trained workers, and so on. The changing needs of capitalism have changed the state. Its pro-capitalist nature remains the same.

THE STATE AS NEUTRAL

As I noted in chapter six, the theory and practice of social democracy is largely based on the supposition that the state is neutral. For the social democrat it is only necessary to elect more and more left-wing MPs into parliament, where by voting and arguing they can use the power of the state to force capitalism to compromise with reform demands. Marxists reject this approach for several reasons. In the first place, it is far too limited. Socialism is not just the present state with a majority of pro-socialist MPs. For a socialist state it is necessary to change a legal system that now favours capitalists to one that favours working people, and it is necessary to restructure the army and the police as well as the civil service and the educational system.

Another danger in the social-democratic approach is that it stands in the way of winning socialism in the first place, because it leads to a strategy of collaboration and compromise with capitalists. If one thinks of the state as a neutral field of parliamentary combat, where different interest groups engage in power politics, then there is a tendency to relate to pro-capitalist legislators not as representatives of an enemy class, but as "fellow politicians" to bargain with in striving for consensus and compromise. If the state is thought of as neutral, then its economic powers are likely to be accepted as attempts to "regulate the economy" for everyone, rather than understood as aids to monopoly. Finally, the social-democratic approach to the state restricts the field of working-class struggle to parliamentary politics, thus ignoring the need to develop other forms of strategy and organization for working people as well. Otherwise the worker can be nothing but a passive observer of parliamentary debate once an election is over.

THE STATE AS MAIN ENEMY

The anarchist approach to the state holds that the state itself is the main enemy to be fought. This approach is based on the experience, which no Marxist ever denied, that among other things, states are instruments of coercion. But it is also based on a theory of human nature and society that Marxists disagree with. Anarchists see political organization and government bureaucracy as the main forces in history, while Marxists see these things as effects of the attempts of

88

dominant classes to administer and protect their economic position in varying and specific conditions. Without going into other points of disagreement between anarchists and Marxists, I would like to indicate the two major objections Marxists have to this kind of approach to the state.

One objection is that anarchism reinforces the viewpoint that pro-socialists should never participate in a capitalist state. Marx, Engels and Lenin all pointed out the foolishness of this approach. To the extent that it is possible to make gains for the working class by being elected to a parliament in a pro-capitalist state, then of course this should be done. What must be avoided is falling into the limitations of the social-democratic view of the state and losing sight of the need to organize working people eventually to rebuild the state in their own interests. Working within an essentially pro-capitalist state can *help* in this organization by making it more difficult for capitalists to use their state to prevent working-class gains. It is also possible to force through genuine working-class reforms.

The second objection to the anarchist approach is that Marxists do not see the existence of the state as the main problem. Indeed, they realize that the working class, itself, needs a state.

SOCIALISM

It would be nice if, having broken the capitalist grip on society, working people could proceed directly to a stateless society where administrative jobs were shared and voluntary, and there was no army or police. However, Marxists recognize that this is unrealistic. The job of reconstructing a society previously geared to capitalist interests, of undoing all the spoilage created by a profit-oriented economy requires a professional state administration. Capitalists who have lost their power (and pro-capitalists who identify with them) have proven many times that they will stop at nothing to regain it, and they certainly have no hesitations about breaking the laws of a socialist society. Foreign capitalist powers have also shown that they will try to destroy socialist countries by military invasions and by subversion. Hence, it is necessary to protect a socialist society with police and military forces.

Under socialism the major means of production are socially owned and controlled, and this control is exercised by means of a state. The socialist state also protects the new society. It differs from the capitalist state in that it serves working-class interests rather than capitalist ones. Marx coined the phrase "dictatorship of the proletariat" to describe the form of state needed for the building of socialism. This phrase has not been adopted by some pro-Marxists, who do not like the suggestion that socialism is a dictatorship; hence I would like to devote some space to this concept.

DICTATORSHIP OF THE PROLETARIAT

I think Marx used harsh language in describing socialism this way because he wanted to draw attention to the fact that no state is neutral. Each exists to defend the interests of a class in a society, and this means acting against the interests of some other class. This is true of the pro-capitalist state, and as Marx foresaw, it is true of the socialist state as well. In this respect *all* states are "dictatorships." The question is not whether they use the power of the state to protect some class interests, but *whose* interests they protect. The phrase "dictatorship of the proletariat" contains two elements essential to Marxism:

(1) that the socialist state is not neutral, but is deliberately built to serve the interests of the working class and its allies,

(2) that the power of the socialist state should be used to defend socialism against attempts by pro-capitalists to overthrow it.

Like all concepts the meaning of the dictatorship of the proletariat expanded as it ceased to be only a concept and became a reality with the construction of actual socialism. The concept became associated with the specific ways that socialism was built in some countries, like the Soviet Union, China and Cuba. Due to the specific conditions these countries had to contend with, socialism had to be won and defended militarily; and one revolutionary political party (the Communist Parties of those countries) bore nearly the entire burden of gaining and building socialism. The former condition created a situation in which socialism was born in an atmosphere of martial law, where many values traditionally associated with electoral democracy were out of place. Because of the second circumstance, nearly all socialist state functions came under more-or-less direct control of the revolutionary party.

I think the reason some Marxists feel uneasy about Marx's phrase is that they see the transition to socialism in modern industrial societies may be quite different from these earlier transitions. For example, in a situation where electoral methods play an important role, a coalition of pro-socialist parties may bring about an end

90

to capitalism. Marx, Engels and Lenin did not use "dictatorship of the proletariat" in such a way as to confine the concept to just one type of socialist transition. However (thanks to anti-Marxist use for the most part), the *phrase* "dictatorship of the proletariat" has come to have a limited meaning, and it may well be correct not to use it. On the other hand, the essential meaning of Marx's idea, which was the need to defend and build socialism by a pro-working class state, is central to Marxism and is surely as historically relevant now as it was when Marx first discussed the subject of socialist transition.

COMMUNISM

Pro-bourgeois political theorists like to believe that society is unthinkable without a state. However, in the Marxist view, states did not exist in early communal society ("primitive communism") and states will cease to exist in the advanced classless society ("communism") which will follow socialism. In early communal society there was no need for a state to protect ruling-class interests, since there were no ruling classes, and there were no professional government personnel or armies. This does not mean that there was no form of decision-making in these societies or that there were no means for self defence. These traditional functions were carried out by a very minor division of labour and without a state bureaucracy.

It is hard for us to imagine what communism will be like. When there are no more class divisions in society, when poverty has been eliminated and human potential allowed to develop unfettered, who can say what kind of society people will create for themselves? One thing that can be said is that there will be no state. As in primitive communism, there will be no need for a state to serve ruling-class interests, since society will not be divided into rulers and ruled. Hard as it may be for some to believe, there will be no need for armies or police forces. It will not be in anybody's interest to wage war. Nobody will need to steal, and society will no longer breed aggressive and crime-prone personalities. There will be no capitalist class to create poverty, and nobody will want to foment a counter-revolution to bring capitalism back, since it will be correctly seen as an unpleasant relic of the human past.

A communist society will not be an unorganized society. Production, education, transportation, scientific research, housing and many other things will obviously need to be organized. Under socialism this is done by members of a professional civil service, selected because they have the necessary ability and education. No doubt under communism people highly trained in specific areas will

91

aid planning by providing expert advice in an organized way, but it will not be necessary, Marxists think, to maintain a group of professional administrators. The level of education under communism will be much higher than under any previous societies, and because of advanced technology it is anticipated that people will have much more free time. Marxists thus suppose that administrative work will be carried on by voluntary peoples' organizations, such as the trade unions, youth groups, community groups and other organizations that are already playing an increasingly important role in governmental administration in socialist countries. Administrative work will be shared by all members of a communist society, and nobody will need to be a lifetime administrator.

How, exactly, might all this work? The question is interesting to contemplate, but since we live at a time when worldwide socialism has not even been secured, the amount that can be said about future societies is necessarily limited.

IS MARXISM UNREALISTIC?

Marxists are often charged with being unrealistic in their views about communism. This charge is sometimes just an expression of the attitude of anti-intellectualism discussed in chapter seven. There is a sceptical rejection of *any* attempt to predict the future course of human history, and such attempts are written off as "wishful thinking."

More often, the charge is based on an elitist conviction that society must always be divided into a few capable of ruling and the majority who are not. This view flies in the face of many examples where supposed "followers" (that is, ordinary working people) organize themselves even when capitalists do everything in their power to stop them. The view also attempts to deny the way human abilities are *created* by their social environment. An important task of socialism seen by Marx and Engels was to train people in the art of self-government, thus laying the groundwork for communism.

Marxists see communism as a society that will evolve out of socialism. As Marx and Engels put it, the state will "wither away" as it ceases to serve any function. This concept has led to another criticism by anti-socialists who claim that under socialism the state bureaucracy itself becomes a "class" that stands in opposition to the rest of the population and will try to prevent a transition to communism so that its members can hold on to their positions of leadership. This view is held both by anarchists, as part of their theory of society and the state, and by pro-capitalists, as part of their anti-socialist propaganda.

There are several things wrong with this view. It promotes an image of socialist state leaders living high off the hog, preying capitalist-like on the labour of others, but not much concrete information is provided to back this image up. There have been a few recent socialist leaders whose biographies are somewhat known in capitalist countries — people like Fidel Castro and (the late) Ho Chi Minh. Their lives do not match this image at all, but have exhibited hard work and many sacrifices. This should lead people to suspect that if they knew the lives of other socialist state leaders they would find that they do not match the "capitalist pig" image either.

Furthermore, it is questionable how "privileged" the place of socialist state leaders is. In the first place, unlike capitalists, they cannot hire people to work for them but must work themselves, often with long hours. In the second place, while we are told that socialist state leaders' salaries and "fringe benefits" put them toward the top of the salary scales in socialist countries, we are not told what the scales are. This is because the spread between the best off and the least well off in socialist societies is very small in comparison with the staggering spread in capitalist societies, where some starve and others are multi-millionaires.

But the main problem with this criticism of Marxism is economic. If socialist state leaders constitute a ruling class with all the power of the state behind them, then why don't they use this power to create privileges like those enjoyed by capitalists? Why aren't they millionaires? When they leave public office, why don't they take fortunes with them? Why don't they secure inheritance rights so as to pass their supposed privileges on to descendants? The reason is that while capitalism is a system in which a few can privately control the main source of power in a society — its means of production — under socialism this is not possible. Major means of production cannot be privately owned, and the misuse of public production administered by state leaders would disrupt a planned economy. They could not turn public means of production to their own personal use, even if they wanted to, without throwing the society into a state of economic chaos. This would not only make the private use of production less useful to them, but it would spark resistance by a population that had already had the experience of one revolution and would not take a return to the old system sitting down.

Sometimes anti-Marxists say that it is not economic privilege

93

that makes socialist state leaders a "ruling class" but a monopolization of political power. Marxists argue in the first place that political power does not exist in a vacuum, but is based on economic power. Second, Marxists maintain that just as the *economic system* of socialism prevents the misuse of the economy to serve special groups, so the *political system* of socialism is essentially democratic.

READINGS FOR CHAPTER EIGHT

F. Engels, *The Origin of the Family, Private Property and the State*. Part IX of this work is a good summary of Engels' view on the state.

V.I. Lenin, *State and Revolution* (in Vol. 25 of the *Collected Works*). This work summarizes the Marxist theory of the state and criticizes reformist and anarchist alternatives.

K. Marx, *Critique of the Gotha Programme*. Here Marx states the need for a working-class state, the "dictatorship of the proletariat.'

Chapter 9

DEMOCRACY

In this chapter I would like to defend a comment Lenin once made that socialism is "a million times more democratic" than capitalism. I realize that this claim runs against what we are told almost daily — that socialism is supposed to be "totalitarian" — and it seems to be refuted by some anti-democratic attitudes and policies that have existed in the histories of socialist countries, such as the USSR during its period of Stalinism. However, in spite of this, and bourgeois propaganda to the contrary, I believe that Lenin's statement is correct.

DEMOCRACY

First of all it is necessary to have a clear idea about what "democracy" and related concepts mean. Probably nothing in bourgeois society is discussed and taught in a more abstract and confusing way. Ideas like "freedom" and "equality" are presented as if they exist in some magical realm of their own, and different states are classified according to whether they are supposed to have somehow come into existence just to defend these abstract values or to thwart them.

Concepts having to do with democracy apply in societies where there are states and hence people who govern and other people who are governed. Such societies are democratic to the extent that the people who are governed have an effective say in how they are governed. In itself this idea is quite simple, and to us today it seems almost obvious that societies should be democratic. But most societies in human history have not been democratic; nor have they advanced democracy as a value. Even when democracy has been promoted as something to be valued, it has been restricted in accord with the needs of a ruling class.

We are told that the idea of democracy was first advanced by the ancient Greeks in Athens. What we are not usually told is that democracy for them meant that male citizens of Athens had a say in government. Women, slaves, immigrants, in short a very large majority of the Athenian population, were excluded. In the early days of bourgeois democratic theory and practice, the situation was similar. John Locke, the influential seventeenth-century English political theorist, also restricted democratic rights to property owners. Not only that, while Locke is famous for being a democratic critic of the old feudal monarchy in England, when he was asked to draft a constitution for one of England's colonies in North America (Carolina), he recommended a feudal-type government which as the constitution put it would "avoid a numerous democracy." The bourgeois class interests Locke favoured were solidly behind democracy *provided* it applied only to some people and only in some places.

Marxists hold that in class-divided society, democracy always involves a say in government *for* the dominant class. Neither capitalism nor socialism is an exception. For the capitalist to have an effective say in how he is governed, that is, in order for him to use the state in his attempt to become rich from the labour of others, he must be able to compensate for the fact that the capitalist class represents a tiny minority of society's population. In capitalist societies capitalists exercise effective self-government by using their money to rig elections, to control political parties, to buy off government leaders, to control the press and other media, and so on. Under socialism, where the dominant class is the working majority, it is made legally and economically impossible for anyone to do these things.

FREEDOM AND EQUALITY

Values associated with democracy like "freedom" and "equality" must also be seen in their specific historical contexts. When early capitalists talked of freedom and equality they meant something very specific. They wanted freedom *from* the state-enforced restraints of the old feudal ruling class on trade and manufacture. They wanted a labour force made up of people who were legally equal in the job market. They conceived of equality in economic terms, where labour power could be bought as needed by capitalists and paid for in accord with the universal standard of labour time. To

LOCKE

provide a large and flexible force to be exploited, capitalists wanted state recognition of these rights.

We are so used to talking about freedom and equality in the abstract that we often lose sight of the fact that it makes a difference *what* freedoms people are supposed to have and *how* they are supposed to be equal. In capitalist societies there is a basic freedom to exploit the labour of others — to be a capitalist. In socialist societies this is not considered a freedom worth protecting at all; in fact it is outlawed. On the other hand, freedom from poverty, unemployment and illiteracy are all considered basic rights in socialist countries, while in capitalist countries these are considered only as privileges or lofty aims to "keep in mind." Much is made of freedom of speech and assembly in bourgeois societies (where you need money to use them effectively), but not much is made of the freedom to *organize* trade unions and other citizen's movements. On the contrary, Canadian labour law and the courts put quite a few obstacles in the way of attempts by working people to organize against the bad effects of capitalism. Similarly, socialists consider economic equality a basic democratic right, while for capitalists economic equality is usually a formal matter — equality before the law. As the French novelist Anatole France puts it in one of his political satires:

> The law in its majestic equality prohibits rich and poor alike from stealing bread, sleeping under bridges, or begging in the streets.

It is for all these reasons that Marxists prefer not to slogan-monger about democracy in vague and abstract terms, but discuss democratic values as they are interpreted and realized in the lives of people under the political rule of different class societies.

DEMOCRACY AND BOURGEOIS RULE

Bourgeois revolutions, like those in England in the seventeenth century and France in the eighteenth, have typically sought to establish parliamentary democracies — governments like our own with elected parliaments and proclaimed commitment to the values of equality and freedom. These governments are advanced in the name of humanity in general, but are in fact designed to serve bourgeois interests. In the histories of bourgeois societies it has become clear that parliamentary democracy is the favoured form of capitalist rule. Why is this? Why do capitalists not prefer to rule through a pro-bourgeois absolute monarch or a military dictatorship? Capitalists have no moral aversion to such regimes, as is proven by their support of them, to protect their imperialist ventures around the world, and by their willingness to turn to fascism when threatened. Current examples include capitalist economic, political and military support for the extreme anti-democratic governments in Chile, South Africa, Taiwan, South Korea and Brazil.

For an explanation of capitalism's preference for parliamentary democracy we need to look at the origins of capitalist rule. One reason the bourgeoisie favoured parliamentary democracy was that in fighting feudal restrictions on trade and manufacture, they had to offer some (false) promise of a share of power to working-class allies, whose help was indispensable to the bourgeois revolutions. Having won these revolutions, capitalists strove to maintain the promise in order to keep popular support.

Another advantage of parliamentary democracy for capitalists is that it is relatively flexible. The problem with relying on a military dictatorship is that it is harder to change this form of government if it starts to do things capitalists do not like. For instance, after a certain point, German capitalists found it impossible to control the Hitler government that they had themselves created. When the Nazis prolonged the war after it was obviously a lost cause, some capitalists were dragged down. By way of contrast, the system of parliamentary democracy in the United States made it possible for capitalists there to get rid of Nixon when he started behaving in a crude and irresponsible way from the point of view of efficiently disguised pro-capitalist government.

Marx noted an important feature of the parliamentary form of government in his analysis of the ill-fated French Second Republic, which lasted from 1848 to 1852, when it was replaced with a military dictatorship. Most obviously in its early stages, capitalism is marked by *competition* among individual capitalist enterprises and groups of enterprises. Even now, capitalists all fight on two fronts: on the one hand they fight against one another for larger profits and for economic survival and on the other hand they fight against other classes in society, most notably the working class. Initially they fought against the remains of feudalism as well. Parliamentary democratic governments are ideal for capitalism, because they provide capitalists with a forum to carry on inter-capitalist conflict without weakening the position of the entire class.

This form of government may be the best for capitalism, but it is not without its problems. Marx's analysis of the fall of the Second Republic hinged on discovering a major contradiction within its democratic government. There were limits to the French bourgeoisie's ability to confine its democratic benefits to itself. Other classes, including the working class, were able to take advantage of democratic forms and safeguards (which after all *in theory* were for everyone) to advance their own positions. Caught in a bind between abandoning democracy altogether or allowing practice to match theory, the bourgeoisie opted for the former with the resulting military dictatorship.

This is a general problem for all bourgeois democracies — how to maintain self-rule and safeguards of equality and freedom for capitalists but not to extend them to other classes. It seems to me that it is impossible to understand the nature and history of bourgeois democracies (or of bourgeois-democratic theories) unless they are seen against the background of this central problem. Let me illustrate what I mean by listing some of the main attempts to solve the problem.

Open limitation of democracy. In their earliest days bourgeois democracies simply excluded large segments of the population from the benefits of democracy openly. Women were denied the franchise. Property ownership was a legal condition for holding public office and for voting, and slavery was permitted. This practice extends to the present in the form of anti-labour and anti-communist legislation, legal discrimination against migrant workers and other limitations. But as the working class of a bourgeois society grows stronger, such open limitation of democracy is harder to maintain.

The facade of formal democracy. Undoubtedly the most effective way of limiting democracy is to maintain it in form, while denying people the means of benefiting from it. Thus it is one thing to have freedom of speech when you own a newspaper or radio station, quite another when you couldn't buy a radio station if you saved half your paycheck for life. Anybody can become Prime Minister or President, but it helps to be backed by millionaires or to be one yourself.

Also, democratic rights and duties are mainly restricted to certain relations between individuals and the government. They do not extend to people's daily work lives. Thus, it is a democratic right to have a say, by voting, in who will become one's M.P. (although few people have a say in who *runs* for M.P.), but working people have no right to a say in how things should be produced in their own places of work.

Lying and cheating. Closely related to the above is the time-honoured method of systematic hypocrisy. It is one thing to endorse a democratic form of government. It is another thing to act accordingly, and if you have enough money it is not very hard to get away with practically anything (unless people with more money object).

Two favoured forms of this hyprocrisy are lying at election time and cheating on taxes. Johnson was elected on a peace ticket in the U.S. and proceeded to initiate most of the military policies in Vietnam advocated by his rival, Goldwater. Trudeau campaigned on the platform that unlike his rival, he would not institute wage and price controls. After being elected he instituted them. (Incidentally, here we have another piece of trickery, because although it was wage and price controls that were instituted, most prices have been allowed to rise while wage increases won in contracts have been slashed almost across the board.)

In a recent survey made by the Swedish trade union newspaper *Aftonbladet,* it was revealed that millionaire industrialists in that country can avoid paying very high taxes. Kapp-Al, a leading chain-store magnate in Sweden, once paid taxes on the equivalent of 7,000 dollars; his maid paid taxes on 9,000 dollars. While hospitals are being closed in Ontario due to "inevitable cutbacks," in 1975 Falconbridge Nickel received a cool eight-million-dollar tax rebate from the Ontario government. This was done in accord with a law (itself never discussed by the people of Ontario), which returned a proportion of taxes provided the nickel was processed in Ontario, presumably to provide jobs. However, by the time of the actual rebate, the clause in the legislation about having to process the nickel in Ontario had been struck out. I'm sure that readers can all provide similar horror stories from their own part of the country.

Compromise and co-optation. As working-class movements become stronger, it is harder to keep pro-working class representatives out of bourgeois parliamentary forums and to prevent the passing of progressive legislation. Sometimes capitalists have no option but to compromise, although they would prefer to do without the labour legislation that favours labour, restrictions on price gouging, and so on. However, some reforms can be accommodated, though uncomfortably, by capitalism. Also, there is always the possibility of co-optation. A combination of bribes and threats can sometimes intimidate working-class backed representatives in a bourgeois parliament into confining themselves to relatively minor reforms. The experience of social democracy has shown that this can be effective even when such representatives form a government.

Kicking over the board. There are limits capitalists will not go beyond. When reforms begin to cut significantly into the profits of the large monopolies and to move in the direction of social revolution; when working-class political forces that cannot be co-opted begin to gain strength; and when the other techniques for limiting democracy fail, capitalists have shown themselves quite willing to throw out democracy altogether in favour of *fascism* — the second-favoured form of capitalist rule.

DEMOCRACY AND SOCIALISM

The very phrase "socialist democracy" is portrayed in capitalist countries as a contradiction in terms. The message is clear: "There may be a lot you don't like about a capitalist Canada, but at least there is democracy here, and you won't have that under socialism." Canadian working people can judge for themselves how much democracy they have now. They can judge the extent to which they determine how they will be governed, how free they are to do what they want and what kind of equality there is in this country. But would the much-proclaimed "horrors" of present-day socialism descend upon us if we "went socialist"?

Many Canadians have the very carefully promoted impression that not only is socialism undemocratic, but that it is fascistic as well. This impression is created in several ways. Without citing facts or figures, Stalinist crimes of over 20 years ago are reported as if they are ongoing and of the same magnitude as fascist campaigns of mass murder and genocide. (The same anti-socialists seldom compare things like the systematic slaughter of the Vietnamese by the U.S. military with Hitler's activities.)

Superficial similarities between fascist and socialist countries are referred to in a dark and ominous way to prove that they have identical state forms. Thus it is emphasized that both fascist and socialist countries have secret police agencies. But so does *every other* country in the world. It is claimed that both are totalitarian because they have one-party systems. Well, some socialist countries do, others don't, and some fascist countries, such as South Africa, have multi-party systems. Therefore, these things do not prove that fascism and socialism are the same.

In fact socialist countries, unlike Canada and other capitalist

101

countries, conduct active legal and educational campaigns *against* the attitudes fascists push, such as racism and worship of irrationality and brute force. Socialist countries have been very successful in providing equal opportunities for their native peoples while fascists typically try to kill them off, and there are many more examples of policies that are the opposite of the things you would expect from fascist states. This is because the political and economic essence of socialism is completely different than that of fascism, as I will argue in this chapter and the next.

The picture of socialism as anti-democratic is wrong on three counts: (1) It distorts the truth about present-day socialism; (2) It ignores the conditions under which socialism has been won and built in the past and under which it can be built in the future; (3) It attempts to obscure the fact that the essence of socialism, unlike any other previous political society, is a movement of the *majority* for self-determination right from the start.

PRESENT-DAY SOCIALISM

The constant stories about socialist countries we hear are mainly lists of supposed restrictions on democracy in those countries. Since the record of the pro-capitalist "news" media is not very reliable insofar as representing the truth in our own society, many Marxists (including myself) are prepared to believe that many of these stories are outright lies. However, even when they are not lies, they distort the truth. This is done in several ways.

The main way is by means of "lies of omission." We are not told about the existence and the power of people's organizations in socialist countries: labour unions, youth and women's groups and a variety of other voluntary organizations which play key roles in running the state. When new legislation is being proposed it is first sent to these organizations to be debated and returned to legislators with criticisms. Voluntary organizations propose legislation, and they advance candidates to run for public office. What is more, these organizations perform some of the tasks that are state functions under capitalism.

In the German Democratic Republic, for instance, as in most other socialist societies, there are trade union courts in which a worker may be tried by his or her own co-workers for civil offences. In Cuba, people's militias, organized on a neighbourhood basis, form the basic units of the military. If democracy means effective people's control over the state, then what is more democratic than people's

102

organizations playing a *direct* role in important parts of the state — the courts and the military? Literature coming from socialist countries gives other examples of people's participation in running the state in present-day socialism. The pro-capitalist "information" media do not deny the existence of these things, but you seldom read about them there either.

Anti-socialist propaganda distorts the truth also by giving only partial information about critical situations. For instance, somebody crossing or attempting to cross the "Berlin Wall," erected in 1961 by the socialist government of the German Democratic Republic, receives front page publicity in the capitalist world. The wall is described as something to keep people from "escaping to freedom." The wall exists, and it is true that some people are denied permission to emigrate from the GDR. But there is much more to the Berlin Wall.

The *primary* purpose in putting up the wall was to stop a U.S.-backed campaign of economic sabotage by the capitalist Federal Republic of Germany. Like all countries devastated by the war, the GDR faced terrible problems building up its farms and industries to provide food and other necessities. As in other socialist countries, these goods were offered at much lower prices than in the capitalist countries of Europe. In a campaign of economic sabotage people were encouraged to go into the GDR and buy up these much-needed goods. This situation had already drained millions of dollars worth of goods out of the GDR each year before it finally constructed a wall to stop it.

This is the most important fact about the Berlin Wall, but it is almost impossible to find it discussed in bourgeois news reports or histories of the wall. Certainly, in the hysterical climate of the West in 1961, there was carefully orchestrated news coverage that completely blacked out any real information on the Berlin Wall. Even now it is difficult to find an account of the GDR's own explanation of why some people are denied permission to emigrate from the country when they want to. (The explanation, in brief, is that those with needed skills are educated entirely at the expense of the people of the GDR. They should use these skills at home rather than accept bribes offered by capitalist countries partly designed to produce a "brain drain.") Nor do bourgeois sources report the number of people who *are* permitted to leave the GDR or the increasing number who, having left, are now returning.

Of course, the issue of the Berlin Wall is a complicated one, and I don't pretend to have discussed all its aspects or to have met all criticisms of it. But the example illustrates the way anti-socialist propaganda selects from a complex situation only those facts it can use to discredit socialism.

Another way to "lie with truths" about socialism is to describe socialism as if things that happen there are completely outside of history. A couple of years ago several books by the pro-feudalist Solzhenitsyn were published all over the capitalist world with much fanfare. In these books Solzhenitsyn describes many anti-democratic events and policies in the Soviet Union (many fictional, but some reports of actual facts). What he and the pro-capitalist commentators on his books failed to mention is that almost all these events took place during the period of Stalinism, some 20 years earlier. Since that time the Soviet Union *itself* has condemned the anti-democratic excesses of Stalinism and has taken measures to prevent its return, such as putting internal police organs under civilian political control.

The treatment of Stalinism by anti-socialists also ignores history by failing to explain the conditions under which Stalinism arose. When the relatively new socialist state was still struggling to emerge from a very poor and still partially feudal society, it was forced into a state of martial law by the various attempts of capitalist states to topple it. These attempts continued without pause right up to the massive invasion of the Soviet Union by Hitler's armies. After the war the USSR had to contend with nuclear blackmail by the USA, which used its monopoly of the atomic bomb from 1946 to 1954 to threaten socialist countries with annihilation. There is no society in the world that could undergo such trials without putting restrictions on democratic procedures. This does not justify the *abuse* of these restrictions during the Stalin period, but it shows that it took extreme circumstances to make them possible. However, in the anti-socialist propaganda Stalinism is made to look like the normal state of affairs in socialist societies.

Yet another way that anti-socialists "lie with the truth" is to report facts about socialism and interpret them with standards the anti-socialists *themselves* set up as absolute measures of democracy. The best example of this is the criticism of socialist societies with one-party political systems. It is *assumed* that only a multi-party system can be democratic (as if being able to choose between two or more pro-capitalist political parties is democratic). It is true that some present-day socialist societies have only one political party. This, incidently, is true also of many new states emerging from national-liberation struggles, and it is not true of all socialist

104

societies, some of which, like Hungary, Poland, the GDR and Bulgaria, have multi-party systems. However, a one-party system is not automatically anti-democratic.

In a society where, for definite historical reasons, only one party emerges as an effective one for gaining and running a new state, then that society can be democratic provided there is democratic access to the party and internal democracy within it. It is for this reason, I believe, that anti-socialist political reports never discuss the way people enter Communist Parties in socialist countries, what the class composition of those parties is, or how decisions are made within them. They do not discuss the democratic process that goes on at the level of nominating candidates, where people's organizations like trade union locals put forward names of those they live and work with and debate their merits before voting on whom to nominate for public office. They write about Communist Parties in socialist countries as if they were the same as the closed cliques of professional schemers who effectively control bourgeois political parties, rather than as democratic mass organizations of working people.

DEMOCRACY AND SOCIALIST ORIGINS

I have already noted that anti-socialist accounts do not explain the conditions that make restrictions on democracy possible and sometimes necessary. If they did, it would be obvious that anti-democratic excesses are not essential to socialism, but are made possible by very extreme circumstances — usually caused by the capitalist countries. It would also show that *some* limitations on democracy have been justified. Socialist Cuba existed for 17 years before having general elections. This was no doubt a limitation on democracy. However, if you take into account the history of the Cuban revolution you can see that it would have been unrealistic to have held elections very much earlier. In the first place, there was the need to eliminate illiteracy and to provide education for people with very little experience of electoral procedures before an election could be a meaningful democratic expression. In the second place, it was necessary to secure the new Cuban society against a relentless attempt of its U.S. neighbour to destroy it. The U.S. tried everything: an economic blockade, a military invasion (the Bay of Pigs), and, as is now a matter of public fact, repeated efforts at internal subversion. In these conditions, an election prematurely held could very well have created the sort of confused political climate that would have been destructive to the efforts to build the new society and, at worst, would have been taken advantage of by the U.S. to restore the fascist regime it had supported before.

By ignoring the conditions under which socialism is gained and constructed, anti-socialists achieve another purpose. They not only keep people ignorant of the difficult conditions that present-day socialist countries faced, but they lead people to overlook the *advantageous* conditions now existing in the industrialized world for winning and building a socialism that is highly democratic right from the start. I have four conditions in mind.

(1) Because socialism in industrial societies will inherit a relatively well-developed economic and cultural potential (factories already built, advanced technology, a large-scale school system), it will not be necessary to sacrifice democratic procedures to the need to build economic strength from scratch or to face general illiteracy.

(2) The changed balance of world forces makes it harder for capitalists to destroy new socialist countries economically and militarily. In 1917 all the combined forces of the capitalist world were able to throw their weight behind a drive to destroy the new Soviet state, because it stood alone. Now capitalists have to contend with many different socialist countries and movements toward socialism. Capitalist forces are being spread more and more thinly. Also, new socialist states can depend on already secure ones for economic help and military protection. This means that though they will surely face dangers and difficulties, new socialist societies may escape the extreme "state of siege" situation in which democratic procedures are often sacrificed.

(3) Modern industrial society is becoming more and more polarized into a few giant monopolies on the one hand and nearly everybody else on the other hand. This has been leading larger and larger segments of the population to organize against the monopolies. Not only the working class, in its industrial and its non-industrial sectors, is included, but also people in the middle classes, the petty bourgeoisie and even some small capitalists. It includes also farmers, student organizations, organizations of racial and ethnic minorities, community and religious groups, and in some countries even parts of the military and police. Eventually all this could lead to a socialist transformation, involving a very large coalition of popular forces, by electoral means. A strong emphasis on democratic policies and respect for democratic procedures among the members of such coalitions is not something to be striven for in a future socialist society, but will be an important weapon against the monopolies from the very start. It will be required to

maintain the unity of these anti-monopoly coalitions and of the broadly-based socialist movements that can grow out of them.

(4) It is important to realize that socialism in a modern society like ours will be won by people who come from a tradition that highly values democracy. The extension of democracy will be as much an initial revolutionary demand as the filling of bellies. What is more, a great many people in our society have had practical experience in some form of self-rule, in school or community groups, in unions or in local government. Therefore they will be educated in the often difficult skills of democratic politics.

SOCIALISM AS A MOVEMENT OF THE MAJORITY

Bourgeois accounts of socialism describe socialist revolutions as the seizure of power by a small minority. However, a study of any socialist revolution shows that this is not the case. Nor could it be the case. Superiority in numbers is one of the main advantages that the working class has over the bourgeoisie. Having achieved socialism, majority support is needed more than ever to build it, since this is not an easy task and is bound to require great effort and sacrifices on the part of the whole population (especially if capitalist countries are still around to throw wrenches into the works).

The fact that the essence of socialism is a movement of the majority makes it different from all previous societies since the early communism of hunting and gathering societies. The ruling class in previous societies sought ways of preventing the majority of the population from effectively determining how they are to be governed. Socialism must find ways of extending democracy, even in the face of hardships that have put many obstacles in the way of developing the full democracy that socialism both makes possible and requires. Socialism faces the problem of how to create a situation where limitations on democratic rights will be least subject to abuse and mistakes and where eventually these limitations can be gotten rid of altogether. I will list some steps that can be taken to solve this problem.

Economic equality. It is important that income differences become minimized as quickly as the demands of building a strong economy permit so that democracy is not merely formal. By eliminating immediately the gross inequalities under capitalism, socialism goes a long way toward this goal. Then the problem is solved further by providing guaranteed jobs, free educational and medical services and ceilings on retail prices and housing costs. It is also important

107

for socialism to democratize the work place so working people have a say in the conditions and outcome of their work.

Education. If people are to have real equality of access to decision-making procedures they must be educated. Not only formal education is required; practical experience in self-rule is needed at the local levels of government and where people live and work. The problem of providing this training has been especially acute in those socialist countries (the majority) that came out of underdeveloped, sometimes feudal conditions.

Combating authoritarianism and bureaucracy. If socialism is built in relatively favourable conditions and people are constantly on guard against the misuse of authority, the development of bureaucratic structures that inhibit democracy should be avoided altogether. It is not surprising that such misuse poses a danger when socialism must be built under conditions resembling a military siege. In these conditions, people are prepared to by-pass checks on anti-democratic tendencies in government bureaucracy. So it is necessary to ensure that elected officials are accountable to the bodies that elect them and government bureaucratic structures and personnel can be criticized and changed.

Separation of party, state and mass organizations. Most socialist revolutions so far have concentrated a very large proportion of power in the hands of Communist Parties, who have assumed the main, and sometimes the sole, role in leading socialist revolutions. Politically experienced people were relatively few in number and concentrated in Communist Parties. Fidel Castro, among others, has discussed the problem arising from this phenomenon.

In his address to the 1975 Congress of the Communist Party of Cuba, Castro described how "confusion of the functions of the Party and those of the state" had been a problem in building Cuban socialism. He also indicated how the party had tended to replace the trade-union movement and other mass organizations. Castro reviewed the work done since 1970 to overcome these problems by delineating the functions of the party, the state and mass organizations.

These sorts of problems will not be so acute for future socialist revolutions in industrialized countries, where socialism can be won and built by coalitions of pro-socialist organizations, and there will be larger pools of literate and trained people to take on governmental jobs and to lead mass organizations. Still, differentiation between the functions of the party, the state and organizations like trade unions is important for spreading power to a broader segment of the population and allowing more people to become trained in self-rule.

The important point about all four of these measures is that they and other measures for extending democracy are ones that can be taken under socialism. There are no *class interests* to prevent these measures from being taken and from being successful. I believe that present-day socialist societies are extending democracy in these ways, with varying degrees of success and not without ups and downs. The crucial question for us is whether in a socialist Canada we could successfully take measures to make that society democratic. I see no reasons why we could not.

I believe we are now in a position to see why Lenin was right in his comparison of socialism and capitalism. The point is not that there is no democracy whatsoever under capitalism. With the bourgeois revolutions democracy was recognized as a value for the first time on a large scale. True, capitalists really wanted it only for themselves and are hypocritical democrats at best. But at least democratic government was generally projected as desirable, and some of the formal requirements of democracy were implemented. Further, there have been some genuine democratic advances for working people under bourgeois rule, not because capitalists wanted it, but because working people did and were powerful enough to force democratic reforms on the bourgeoisie. Nor is it denied that the democratic development of existing socialist societies has sometimes been seriously open to criticisms. Grave mistakes and even crimes have been committed in the building of socialism.

Rather, the point is that capitalism and socialism have radically different problems. If capitalism is going to continue to have the free rein it needs to exploit working people and to plunder the world, it must find ways keep working people from participating in government. If socialism is to succeed it must continue to remove impediments to thorough-going democracy. Capitalism may have laid the formal groundwork for democracy, but its problem is to *limit* real democracy. Socialism provides the basis for real democracy and has the problem of *extending* democracy. For capitalism to survive democracy must be curtailed. For socialism to survive and to develop, democracy must be constantly extended. That is why socialism is "a million times more democratic" than capitalism.

109

V. I. Lenin, *Proletarian Revolution and the Renegade Kautsky,* in Volume 28 of the *Collected Works.* Lenin contrasts bourgeois and proletarian democracy.

K. Marx, *The 18th Brumaire of Louis Bonaparte.* Marx's analysis of the fall of the bourgeois democratic 2nd Republic in France.

For book lists of up-to-date material published by socialist countries in English and available in Canada explaining and defending the democratic nature of their systems, it is best to write to: Progress Books, 71 Bathurst Street, Toronto, Ontario. This is the major Canadian distributor of literature from socialist countries.

Chapter 10

FASCISM

A military officer from Uruguay, unable to tolerate the brutal policies of the military government there, wrote a letter that was published in the April, 1976, *Bulletin* of Amnesty International. His letter says:

> The Uruguayan armed forces systematically torture and maltreat political or trade union detainees. I have hundreds of proofs, from my own painful personal experience. Dozens of prisoners have been taken to the Military Hospital with fractures and lesions. Such a level of sadism has been reached that military doctors supervise the torture.

This is especially alarming when you consider that as of March of 1976 there were an estimated 6,000 political prisoners in Uruguay, a ratio of one prisoner for every 450 citizens. The number of political prisoners and their treatment in Uruguay would be bad enough if it were an isolated occurrence. But it is *typical* of the sort of thing that is official government policy under the state form of fascism.

Fascism is so inhuman it is hard to contemplate. How could a government set out to starve and gas to death all Jewish people as the Nazis attempted in fascist Germany? Where do states like this come from and how can they be prevented? Those questions are not just ones of painful history, since there are still fascist regimes in the world today that carry on brutal acts of repression.

FASCISM AND CAPITALISM

Bourgeois political theorists like to describe socialism and fascism as

111

similar forms of "totalitarianism," equally opposed by the "free" capitalist world. In fact, fascism is a *form* of capitalist rule. From the 1930s when giant corporations like the Ruhr Steel Trust and Krupp Armaments supported the Nazis in Germany and the Mitsubishi conglomerate supported fascism in Japan, right up to the present when ITT was exposed for its role in overthrowing the democratically elected government in Chile for a fascist military dictatorship, there has not been a single example of a fascist state that has not been backed by capitalists.

Classical examples of fascism in its full-blown form include the Italy of Mussolini and the Germany of Hitler. In these places there were all the central characteristics of fascist rule: a movement with a certain mass appeal built up on wild demagogy, inflamed national chauvinism and racial intolerance, violence at home and aggression abroad — all this in support of extreme anti-democratic government. Present-day fascisms sometimes differ from these examples and also among themselves in various ways. For instance, while German and Italian fascism had large fascist political parties to support them, Chile, Uruguay and Thailand depend almost entirely on externally supported military rulers.

South Korea has a parliamentary assembly, although it is virtually powerless, while most fascist states dispense with any semblance of parliamentary rule. Something *approaching* democratic advantages exists for some within the small white populations of South Africa and Rhodesia, while the Black majorities live under a most blatant form of fascism. Despite these differences, there have, unfortunately, been enough examples of fascism in the world so far for us to recognize what it does.

Fascism employs an overt and highly terroristic dictatorship against the overwhelming majority of the population; it systematically disbands and oppresses people's organizations such as trade unions, peace organizations, even neighbourhood groups and professional organizations; it actively promotes an ultra-conservative ideology including racism, national chauvinism, sexism, anti-intellectualism and just about any other bad attitude you can think of. Under fascist rule civil liberties are non-existent. Parliamentary assemblies, where they are allowed to exist at all, are a sham. Military occupation of schools and work places, detention without trial, massive internal spy and informer networks and systematic use of torture are all commonplace.

Sometimes fascists have cynically advanced their programs as

FASCISM

forms of socialism in order to attract people who don't like big business. (The word "Nazi" in German is short for "National Socialist.") Fascist military juntas like to describe themselves as apolitical, neither pro-socialist nor pro-capitalist. In fact, all fascist states have made socialism their first and main targets. In the first *hours* of gaining sufficient power, fascists outlaw Communist and other pro-socialist movements, ban their literature, jail and execute pro-socialists and anybody even suspected of associating with them. None of these things are done to pro-capitalists, and the profits of the largest capitalist enterprises in fascist countries typically rise. It is no accident that on the same days the news sections of Canadian papers were carrying stories about the brutal fascist coup in Chile, their business pages were reporting renewed interest in investment there by U.S. and Canadian corporations.

Whatever fascist leaders say, fascism has never been opposed to capitalism. The Provisional Supreme Economic Council appointed during the reign of the Nazis in Germany included Krupp von Bohlen (armaments manufacturer), Fritz Thyssen (of the German Steel Trust), F.C. Von Siemens (electrical industry), F. von Schroeder (banker), A. Diehn (Potash Syndicate director). These were no anti-capitalist little guys. The personal fortune of Thyssen, for instance, was estimated to be $30,000,000 (in 1935 currency) at the time, and the capital interest of the German Steel Trust he headed was $700,000,000.

In the first two and a half years of fascism in Chile, world capitalist banking centres extended the military junta over one billion dollars in loans. The U.S. sends regular shipments of arms there, some of which, it was recently revealed, are shipped through Canada. From December 1973 to May 1975 the Canadian government and Canadian banks extended around half a billion dollars in loans to the fascist government in South Korea. (Some of this money was used to purchase Canadian nuclear reactors of a sort suitable for making bombs.) These stories do not represent isolated examples of capitalist support of fascism, but are similar to reports of such aid regarding every fascist regime in the world.

THE NATURE AND ORIGIN OF FASCISM

Fascism is a specific form of political rule, and it is important to understand why some countries go fascist. Hence it is important not to confuse fascism with capitalist oppression in general. The latter takes place also under parliamentary democracy, which is a separate political form. Similarly, it is important not to identify fascism with one or another of its features. For instance, state promotion of national chauvinism, racism or sexism does not by itself make that state a fascist one.

Several theories have been advanced to explain the rise of fascism in our century. Two of the more popular explanations are that fascism is the result of frustration on the part of the petty bourgeoisie and the lumpenproletariat (the chronically un-employed and down and out) and that it is the result of social-psychological phenomena such as a widespread need for an authoritarian leader.

These explanations may go some way toward explaining the origin of *fascists*, but they do not explain the origin of *fascism* as a dominant political form. It is true that the ranks of fascist political movements have been filled by members of the petty bourgeoisie and the lumpenproletariat, and authoritarian leaders have apparently appealed to many who have supported the rise of fascism. But there have always been members of these groups who have been frustrated and people with authoritarian hangups. What needs to be explained is why fascism arises as a social force capable of drawing on these groups and feelings.

One explanation given by some liberals is that Communism causes fascism, that if Communism is allowed to become strong, then fascism will arise as a counterforce. It is certainly true that fascists viciously combat Communism, but this does not mean that the latter is the cause of the former. Fascists are not just anti-communists, as liberals and non-communist socialists have discovered when fascism has turned on them as well. But it is no accident that the rise of fascism often accompanies the growth of Communism and other progressive movements. Marxists explain fascism as the abandonment of parliamentary democracy by monopoly capitalists in the face of mounting economic problems and growing people's movements.

Fascism is the second-favoured form of capitalist rule. It is adopted when joint rule among capitalists through parliamentary democracies becomes impossible and dissent among working people is sufficiently widespread to challenge the capitalist system itself. In Germany in the early 30s, for instance, economic crisis had produced high unemployment, lower wages and general economic instability. Worker militancy increased; the Communist Party grew.

114

It was clear that the Weimar Republic, a pro-capitalist parliamentary democracy, was failing to stem a revolutionary tide.

It was at this point that capitalists began supporting the Nazis, and only after this support began did Nazi membership and strength begin to rival that of the Communists and other socialists. In a confidential bulletin of the Federation of German Industry (the *Deutsche Führerbriefe*) leading industrialists actually carried on a correspondence debating the merits of attempting to save the republic or abandoning it and supporting the Nazis. Fascism is a response to capitalism's worst problem: a growing militant people's movement for socialism.

THE SOCIAL PSYCHOLOGY OF FASCISM

While Marxists reject purely psychological explanations of the origin of fascism as a political system, it is important to have some understanding of the social-psychology of fascism. Capitalists opt for fascism because it protects their profits and their profit-making system. Also they personally do not have to get their hands bloody, since this task is entrusted to their fascist thugs. But why do some humans, with little or no economic stake in the capitalist system, become active fascists or passive accomplices? The question is not merely academic, since fascists have been successful in launching propaganda campaigns to gather some popular support for their organizations.

It is important to note that fascist movements always present themselves as mass people's movements. This is crucial to their success. As the wealth and power of a society come to be concentrated in fewer and fewer hands, increasing numbers of people are made to feel trapped and powerless, and in fact they *are* trapped and powerless. This is especially true of many in the petty bourgeoisie and the lumpenproletariat, who can find no way of fighting against big monopoly. It is also true of those sections of the working class who have no organized way of defending their interests. In these circumstances fascism seems to offer the strength of a mass organization to fight back against real and imagined enemies.

Of course, when fascism is sufficiently strong to swing into action it does not really help these people. It often turns on those of them who had believed the promise that it really would combat the big monopolies as well as the "communist menace." The real targets of fascism, of course, are not the monopolies, but the people's

115

organizations that combat monopoly: the trade unions, Communist and other pro-socialist parties, and democratic organizations of all kinds. It is against these organizations, which really do represent people's interests, that fascism launches its brutal campaigns.

Which brings us to a very difficult, psychological question. Why in the face of danger do some people turn to the specific inhuman opinions and practices of fascism? Part of the explanation must be that life under capitalism is itself dehumanizing. Capitalism lays the groundwork for some people embracing a program of action based on blind violence. Competition for jobs, unemployment, insufficient wages to lead a comfortable and happy home life — all these things are themselves forms of violence and they in turn breed violence. The "entertainment" and news media promote a cult of violence and encourage an anti-intellectual culture and a conservative ideology that glorifies irrationality. Further, capitalism lays the groundwork for the typically fascistic divide-and-conquer tactics among people by racial and national persecution.

THE ANTI-FASCIST STRUGGLE

There are two lessons to be learned from the history of fascism and anti-fascist struggles: that fascism should not be *overestimated* and that it should not be *underestimated*. Some on the left (also on the right) hold that fascism is inevitable. In fact, some leftists even hold that it is desirable, since it rips the mask of democratic respectability from the face of capitalism, thus making people more susceptible to revolutionary mobilization. It is true that in turning to fascism, capitalists give up any pretence of democracy and provide a bitter lesson for many, but anyone who has ever experienced life under actual fascism, trying to organize progressive movements, knows how hairbrained this theory is.

Fascism can and must be prevented, which requires in the first place complete unity against fascism among those who otherwise disagree politically. The left (both Communist and non-Communist) learned this lesson the hard way in the 1930s in Germany, where disunity helped the rise of fascism and allowed the Nazis to pick off people's movements one at a time. The press and educational systems can and should be pressured to publicize the truth about fascism and stop confusing people about its nature. Governments should be pressured to stop giving diplomatic, economic and military aid to fascist regimes in other countries. Military and police forces, which usually form the backbone of fascist states, should be

116

brought under democratic public supervision and control. The police and courts must be made to enforce present legislation against fascist groups, and new legislation must be passed against the forming of these groups and the spreading of their literature.

Bourgeois theorists often picture political changes as if they are like changes in the weather — outside of human control and hard to anticipate. But this is not how it works. The groundwork for fascism is laid in bourgeois parliamentary democracy, and there are usually warning signs that can be recognized. Bourgeois democracy can make fascism possible by limiting people's civil liberties. This takes the form of: limits on the ability to organize and to voice complaint against injustices; allowing police and military agencies to harass individuals and organizations (in ways now familiar to Canadians since the disclosure of RCMP spying and "dirty tricks"); and legal discrimination against minority and political groups, thus making it possible to intimidate people in these groups and to divide them from one another and the rest of society. All these things must be recognized and resisted before it is too late.

FASCISM AND CIVIL LIBERTIES

Some anti-fascists see a dilemma here. They reason that if civil liberties must be protected, then so must the civil liberties of fascism itself and of those who advocate fascist values, such as race hatred. Marxists maintain that this way of thinking, however well motivated, makes the mistake discussed in the last chapter of regarding democratic values only in the abstract, rather than taking account of how they work in real life.

In a card game everybody should have a turn to deal. Fair enough. But nobody would complain if the deal were denied to a person when it was known in advance that he planned to use it to cheat or to tear up the cards. Nobody objected when, at the end of World War Two, the allied powers that defeated Nazi Germany imposed a law on the German people denying them the right to form or to advocate forming another fascist political party like the one that had just initiated the worst bloodbath in history up to that time. Too bad such a law had not been made and enforced about 12 years earlier. (Indeed, it is too bad that such a law is not enforced *today* in capitalist "West Germany," where fascist groups and ideas are again on the rise.)

Hitler is said once to have promised the children of his sympathizers: "We will create a youth from which the world will recoil in

117

horror." Obviously groups that try to make good on promises like this should be stopped. Fascists are not interested in airing their views for general debate, recommending them for rational consideration. They need platforms to mobilize people like themselves who have been made incapable of rationality, and history has painfully taught us what they want to mobilize them for.

In their view that some rights (like the right to organize) should not be extended to fascists, Marxists are sometimes charged with undermining civil liberties. Where, the critics ask, do you "draw the line"? Contrary to anti-Marxist propaganda, Marxists do not say that civil liberties should be denied to everyone who disagrees with them. What Marxists do say is that in exceptional cases restricting certain rights is unavoidable to prevent disastrous consequences. In actual practice it is possible to determine what these cases are — for example the laws mentioned above were intended to prevent the rebuilding of Nazism after World War Two. In fact it is largely because Marxists value civil liberties that they want to stop fascism. To this end Marxists warn that stubborn and short-sighted defence of *abstract* principles can result in the destruction of *real* civil liberties.

THE DANGER OF FASCISM

There are two ways that the danger of fascism is underestimated. One is to say that it can't happen here. The other is to say that the issue does not now exist because the conditions for fascism are not yet present in Canada, so it is "paranoia" to raise it. These are both dangerous views.

Fascism can come to Canada just as it has come to several countries with similar economies and parliamentary governments (as for example Chile). Fascism is a form of state adopted by capitalists when they are in trouble, and the capitalists — both foreign and domestic — who run Canada are increasingly troubled. (Indeed, something approaching fascism already has come to Canada in the Duplessis regime in Quebec.) Fascist groups exist in every major city in this country, and their numbers may swell if Canada continues to be a haven for fascist refugees, who seem to have rather an easy time getting through immigration. The military and police forces at all levels of government are generally to the right of centre politically, and are not subject to public review or control. All these conditions are ones that can lead to fascism.

Suggesting that it is premature to worry about fascism misses the point of what an anti-fascist struggle is. The aim is to mobilize people from different walks of life and with different political view-

118

points *now,* so as to prevent fascism *later.* In addition, this opinion overlooks the speed with which capitalism can swing to fascism when it decides to. What today are in the main small and insignificant groups of racist misfits and sadists can tomorrow become large and well-armed organizations. The military and the police can very quickly become concerned about "the inability of civilians to govern themselves." All it takes is a decision on the part of a few of the large monopolies to put their enormous economic support behind fascism.

Imposing the War Measures Act in October, 1970, was not a fascist coup in Canada, but a cynical maneuver on the part of the Trudeau government to weaken the left in Quebec and to frighten people away from separatism and from socialism. However, there is a lesson to be learned from that experience. When Canadians went to bed on October 15, we enjoyed the freedom of assembly, the right not to be held without charge, freedom of the press and all the rest of the civil liberties the government is sworn to preserve. When we woke up the next morning, the War Measures Act had been invoked, none of these rights applied to us, and Quebec was under military rule. That's how fast it could happen here.

READINGS FOR CHAPTER TEN

Palmiro Togliatti, *Lectures on Fascism* (New York, New World Paperbacks, 1976). Togliatti, an important early leader of the Italian Communist Party, gave these lectures in 1935.

Georgi Dimitrov, Speeches delivered at the 7th World Congress of the Communist International, July-August, 1935. These speeches are reprinted in various pamphlets, sometimes titled, "The United Front Against Fascism," or "For Unity of The Working Class Against Fascism;" they are also available in collected works of Dimitrov in libraries and progressive bookstores. In these speeches Dimitrov, a Bulgarian Communist, criticized sectarianism and discussed ways to fight and prevent fascism.

The economic facts about Nazi Germany and about the *Deutsche Führerbriefe* are taken from R. Palme Dutt, *Fascism and Social Revolution* (New York, 1935). This book is out of print, but available in some libraries.

Chapter 11

MATERIALISM

A person's "philosophy" is his or her viewpoint about the nature of the world and about human nature. Everybody has a philosophy, even if it is not very well thought out. Philosophies are part of the superstructure of society and as such they reflect class interests. Under present-day capitalism some leading philosophical ideas are: There is probably a God and humans are not entirely physical. There are no laws in human history. And nobody can really know the truth about anything. Marxists disagree on all three points. They maintain that these and other typical bourgeois philosophical views serve capitalists' interests, while Marxist philosophy is in accord with working people's experience and serves working-class interests.

When first working out their philosophy, Marx and Engels drew upon science and the pro-scientific aspects of previous philosophers. Marxism differs from all other philosophies in being both *materialistic* and *dialectical*. In this chapter I will discuss three theories central to Marxist "materialism"' (1) the universe and everything in it is physical; (2) there are laws of cause and effect which determine what happens in human society and history; and (3) humans can gain objective knowledge about themselves and the rest of the world.

Marxists and other materialists have given many arguments in favour of materialism and in opposition to the views of anti-materialists. I will not reproduce these arguments here, since that would require a book in itself. Those who wish to pursue this topic will find references at the end of the chapter. Instead, I will summarize materialism and show how it differs from an anti-materialist perspective.

121

To hold that everything is material is to deny the existence of a God and non-physical things like human souls. Materialists claim that the physical universe has always existed. Hence there is no reason to suppose it needed to be created by a God. They also hold that humans are physical beings in a physical world. Humans do not possess spiritual souls, but differ from other creatures because, through evolution and social labour, they have acquired some superior abilities, such as the use of language and abstract thought.

Materialists argue that since their view of the world is in accord with everyday experience and the findings of science, there are no good reasons to believe in God or the soul. In fact, many religious theorists now *agree* with materialists on this last point and say that belief in God or the soul is not based on *reason* but on "faith." Marxists see this as an admission that these people cannot give any good reasons for believing their anti-materialist views.

It is often charged that materialism is a debasing, inhuman perspective. It is said that if there were no God or no souls then there could be no morality and life would be without meaning or purpose. One reason that many think that materialism is debasing is that they mistake the philosophical theory of materialism for "crass materialism." This is just a confusion of words. Philosophical materialism is a general theory about the nature of things. "Crass materialism" describes a life style based on selfish greed for material possessions and on short-sighted self-indulgence. Most philosophical materialists, and all Marxists, reject this life style and want to build a world where nobody is a crass materialist.

Materialism and morality. Religious theorists often argue that someone who is an atheist, that is, who believes there is no God, could not be a moral person. They claim that without the promise of divine reward or punishment for acting morally or immorally, there would be no basis for that person's morality. There are some problems with this argument. In the first place, there are many people who are atheists but lead moral lives, and there are religious believers who are not moral. (To say, as some do, that these atheists cannot *really* disbelieve in God, since if they did, they wouldn't be moral, or that immoral people cannot *really* be religious, begs the question by assuming what the critics of atheism want to prove.)

In the second place, Marxists say that there *is* a non-religious basis for morality — namely *humanism.* Morality is a social matter.

Moral rules (like ones that say you should not kill or rob other people) indicate how people ought to act when their actions have effects on other people. In the Marxist view, people are moral to the extent that they act in *cooperative* ways — in ways to avoid harming other people and to help them if possible. This moral code is entirely worldly. It does not require a divine command to justify people's believing it. It is justified by the fact that the survival and progress of the human species requires that people act cooperatively.

Some atheists charge that religion is anti-humanistic in its very nature. Marx and Engels did not share this attitude. Religion, as Marx once put it, can be "the heart of a heartless world." Still, Marxists see limits to a religious basis for morality. When both opposing sides in a war are assured by their religious leaders that they are in the right and the other side in the wrong, it becomes difficult to know which religious interpretations of morality to trust.

The same problem confronts the view that people need fear of punishment or promise of reward in an afterlife in order to be moral. How do you tell *what* is going to be punished and what is going to be rewarded? Moreover, in a humanistic morality, people are considered moral to the extent that they are motivated by a sincere desire to act in a cooperative way. People who act morally only because they fear punishment if they do not, or hope for personal rewards if they do, are not seen by the humanist as very moral people. This is the same whether the rewards and punishments in question are thought to be earthly or other-worldly.

Meaningful life. It is often claimed that life would have no meaning if people were entirely physical. Why not? Suppose that someone sets out to do work that is both rewarding in itself and provides a comfortable life, to find love and companionship and to help build a better world for future generations. Suppose further that this person succeeds, or even just partially succeeds in doing these things. Would the person not have led a meaningful life? What more does there need to be to a meaningful life than to attain goals that are both morally worthwhile and personally satisfying? This does not require a divine plan or an afterlife.

I believe many people think that there must be some supernatural force that makes life meaningful, because it is very difficult to lead a meaningful life in a class-divided society. Even the most basic aims of people are thwarted. Someone works hard for a lifetime to save for old age, and inflation takes away all the savings.

People make sacrifices to gain an education, and there are no jobs requiring the skills they have learned. The "good life" is pictured as owning a house, a car and a TV (plus other expensive things). But the good life turns out to be a lemon. The house and car start falling apart from the day they are purchased, and the TV bombards people with boring mind rot. Is it any wonder that people ask "What is the point of all this?" and look for some other-worldly meaning?

DETERMINISM

Determinism is the position that there are causes for everything that happens. This is true, the determinist holds, not only of lifeless objects, plants and other animals, but also of humans. Marxists are committed to determinism, because they aim to discover laws of cause and effect in society and history. We have already noted some of these laws: that changes in a society's economic base ultimately cause changes in its superstructure; that capitalist competition causes the collectivization of labour; that threatened capitalism tends toward fascism; that the capitalist need for markets and cheap labour causes imperialism; and so on. It is by discovering such laws that Marxists can identify the main sources of problems in society and hence be in a position to help change things.

Discovering causes sometimes requires very hard scientific work. Causes are not always obvious, and they are always complex. There is always more than just one factor involved in the causal history of anything. For instance, it took most of an entire chapter of this book just to sketch in the barest outline the main factors involved in capitalist competition and its effects. Still, natural scientists have been most successful in discovering causes in nature, and Marxists claim they have already discovered many important causes in human society.

Some anti-materialist philosophers argue that there are no causes either in nature or in human history, but most are prepared to grant that everything that happens outside of the realm of humans has a cause. Some are also prepared to grant that there may be *social* and *historical* causes of the kind Marx and Engels discovered, but that on the level of individual human decisions, there are no causes.

This position does not make sense. Human society and history are made up of individual human beings and things they produce. Whatever happens in society and history must therefore involve human decisions and actions. People may not always be aware of the causes of their thoughts and actions, and things do not always work out as they think they will. But as Marx once put it: "the social history of men is always the history of their individual development. . . ." If determinism were not true of individuals, it would not be true of human society and history as a whole. This is why anti-Marxist philosophers sometimes argue that Marxism cannot be correct as a social theory on the grounds that individual human decisions are not caused.

It might be thought that some people reject the idea of determinism regarding individual humans, because they cannot discover causes of their own and other people's ideas and actions, while they do understand causes in the rest of nature. I do not think this is the reason. In our everyday lives, we all know at least some of the causes for people acting and thinking as they do. We know that if we say certain kinds of things to friends or relatives, or even to strangers, they will become angry, that saying other kinds of things will make them sad, and so on. We know that if we change jobs, or if we are laid off, or if our hours of work are changed, it will have definite effects on our moods and our behaviour. We know that if we eat or drink certain things it will affect our attitudes and behaviour in certain ways. In fact, we all have quite a bit of cause-effect knowledge about humans. If we did not, we could not function in our day-to-day lives.

While people can see that their decisions are caused by their own conscious reasons for making them, they sometimes find it hard to understand that there are other, more remote causes for their having these reasons. But think back to some important decision you made in the past — for instance, to change jobs, to quit school or not to quit school, to get married or not to marry, to have children or not, to buy something that would put you in debt. Looking back on it you can usually see at least some of the causes that resulted in your making the decision you did, even if at the time you were not aware of these causes.

I believe that the main reason why many people resist the philosophical position of determinism is that they think it is incompatible with human freedom and that it leads to fatalism and passivity.

Freedom. The word "freedom" is one of those words used by pro-bourgeois writers to stand for everything socialists and Marxists are supposed to be against. Of course, if "being free" is taken to mean

125

"acting without any causes," then freedom and determinism are opposed by definition. But anti-determinists usually try to link up the *political* sense of freedom discussed in chapter nine with the philosophical debate over determinism. The suggestion is that determinism is incompatible with people's freedom of action. Therefore someone who believes in determinism will be prepared to go along with political constraints on people's personal freedoms.

If freedom means the ability to do or say what you want, then determinism is not at all incompatible with freedom. Whether what a person wants or does not want is determined does not diminish his ability to do or say what he wants to do or say. *Why* he wants to do or say these things is another matter.

What is more, determinism makes freedom possible. If you are going to be free, then you have to remove blocks to your doing or saying what you want to. The best way to do this is by understanding the *causes* of these blocks so you know how to remove them and prevent them from returning. For instance, if freedom for working men and women of all races and nationalities is ever to be won, then the attitudes of racism, sexism and national chauvinism must be eliminated. But, as was argued in chapter five, to do this, it is necessary to discover the causes of these attitudes.

The mention of determinism usually brings forth cries of "mind control" by anti-determinists. They say that determinism would lead to attempts to manipulate people's values and ways of thinking. Marxists reply that of course people's values and ways of thinking are determined, and it is a good thing to determine them consciously. For instance, it is a good thing to do what we can to raise our children to have humanistic values and useful knowledge, but we cannot do this without causing them to acquire certain values and beliefs.

The view that it is always "mind control" or "manipulation" to cause people to have certain attitudes is incorrect. Manipulation involves causing people to acquire certain beliefs without their knowing that you are doing this, and usually for selfish motives of your own. Capitalists pay millions of dollars to advertisers to attempt to manipulate people. Pro-capitalist news and educational institutions devote much effort to manipulating people's beliefs about socialism. But causing people to believe things does not have to be manipulation. For example, when you present an argument to somebody you disagree with, you are hoping that you will cause that person to change some beliefs. But this is not manipulation. Nor is it

126

manipulation when you go to a lecture or enroll in a night course expecting that *your own* beliefs or values may be different as a result. Manipulation is not a question of whether people's views are caused, but of how they are caused and for what. It is, in fact, an *exercise* of freedom for people to determine their views themselves.

Fatalism. Another common criticism of determinism is that if the determinists were correct, then there would be no reason for anybody to make a conscious effort to *do* anything. If all our thoughts and actions are determined, then why not just wait until whatever is determined to happen happens? In particular, those who want socialist revolution should not waste their efforts and take risks, but should just twiddle their thumbs until the revolution occurs as it is determined to do. The result of believing determinism, it is urged, would therefore lead to passive inactivity.

The fact that some of the most active people in history — not least of whom were Marx, Engels and Lenin — have been determinists shows there must be something wrong with this argument. In fact, a practising anti-determinist might be the one who is incapable of activity. Not believing in causes, he would not be able to predict the effects of any of his own words or actions on other people. Anything at all might happen no matter what he said or did. Therefore, why should he say or do anything? It would make no difference to what happens in the future whether he acted carefully and deliberately, or thrashed out in any direction depending on his whims at the moment, or did nothing at all.

This criticism of determinism confuses the position of all determinists with that of only a few determinists, called "fatalists." Fatalism is the view that what humans think and feel makes no difference to what happens. A fatalist sees things like human values, plans, theories and desires as nothing but *effects* of something else in history, never as themselves causes. Some fatalists have held that what happens to humans is entirely a result of unconscious biological drives, others that it is a result of geography, others that it is a result of the stars. Marxists are sometimes said to be fatalists who think that people's economic circumstances are the only things that are causes in human society and history.

The truth is that like most other determinists, Marxists reject fatalism. Marxists see human attitudes and desires as important causes in history. Scientific thinking is part of the cause of changes in the forces of production. The competitive and profit-hungry values of capitalists are part of the causes of exploitation and imperialism. Working people's cooperative values are part of the cause of their organizing against capitalism. Marx and Engels saw their own role as social scientists attempting to develop a theory of human society for helping to bring about socialism. For the Marxist events in history happen not in *spite* of what people do, but *because* of it. Once people realize that conscious human thought and action are an essential part of history, then they can hardly think or act on the supposition that "history" will somehow make things happen without them.

What about these important human thoughts, values, and actions themselves? Do they not have causes which, if you go back far enough, people are just born into? Of course. There are social causes for working people coming to have cooperative values and wanting to get rid of capitalism and for capitalists having competitive values. There were causes for Marx and Engels holding and advancing the theories they did. Had Marx or Engels lived 200 years earlier it is virtually impossible that they would have had the same values and advanced the same theories, and of course neither of them had any control over when he was born. These considerations have led some anti-determinists to claim that determinism is fatalistic after all, even if it does allow some role for human consciousness in history.

Why should the fact that our values and beliefs are caused lead to fatalism? They are still *our* values and beliefs. Imagine a boss trying to end a strike by telling his employees: "See here, you know your militant attitudes are caused by having to work in an industrialized and exploitative society, and if you had lived a few hundred years ago, you wouldn't want to go on strike, or even know what a strike is." This would not lead the striking workers to stop having the beliefs or values they do, and it wouldn't slow down the strike for one second.

Although we have no choice over when we are born, and therefore our own control over what our beliefs and values will be is limited, we can expand the amount of control we have. People's attitudes are determined by such things as where and how they live, how they are raised, how they work, whether they are literate and what educational and cultural facilities are available to them. In class-divided society these things are largely determined by the needs of an oppressive ruling class to maintain its rule. Marxists aim to help create a society where these things are under the conscious control of the people themselves.

Marxists maintain that by careful use of our perceptual organs and our ability to reason, we are able to arrive at beliefs about things as they actually are. That is, Marxists hold the view that "objectivity" is possible. Anti-objectivist philosophers claim that we cannot arrive at true beliefs about things, or if we can, we cannot know *when* we have. Some philosophers — "sceptics" — argue that we can have *no* well-founded beliefs about anything. Others claim that there are *some* things we can never know. They grant that objectivity is possible regarding nature, but not regarding human society. There has been a shift in much pro-bourgeois thinking on this point. At one time anti-Marxist philosophers said that Marxism is false. Now more and more of them say that nobody can know what is true or false about human societies. I believe that this is a response to the success of Marxist-led movements, which have made bourgeois thinkers less sure of themselves than they once were.

Anti-objectivists have devoted a lot of time to producing ingenious arguments to show that objectivity is impossible. Taken in the abstract, some of their arguments can seem convincing. However, Marxists maintain that the incorrectness of anti-objectivism is illustrated by an examination of actual human practice. Humans do not act on blind instinct, but on conscious beliefs. In order to survive and to progress, we need to have true beliefs about our environment and about other people. If these beliefs could only be true by accident, then it would be impossible for the species to have survived, much less to have built huge cities, sent people to the moon, organized trade unions or community groups, carried out social revolutions, or done any of the other things that require careful and accurate planning.

Some non-Marxists have advanced a very rigid and unrealistic view of what objectivity is, which may lead some people, including some who otherwise favour Marxist theories, to reject the possibility of objectivity. If someone thinks that objectivity means that you can always trust first appearances, then it would be a very weak position indeed. Marx's own work required him to dig beneath appearances and discover the underlying workings of class struggle in society. Similarly, objectivity is not the same thing as *certainty*. You can hold some beliefs objectively and still be prepared to admit that you may be mistaken and will have to change your views if new facts come to your attention.

Bias. Some suggest that objectivity requires complete neutrality, so

129

only somebody with no concern at all about the outcome of an inquiry could be objective. This is also a mistaken view of objectivity. Marxists agree that ivory-tower impartiality is a myth. Marx and Engels were quite good at showing how social scientists have deep class interests in the outcome of their work, even if they present themselves as being completely neutral.

Anti-objectivists often confuse being *partisan* with being *biased*. To be partisan is to have some interest at stake in an inquiry, to *care* how it comes out. Marx and Engels cared about their own inquiry. Marxism is an entirely partisan theory. It is partisan to the interests of the working class. Marx supported socialism only because he considered it in the interest of the working class. To be biased, on the other hand, is to be so blindly committed to a position that you cannot recognize facts that contradict it, or you cannot reason properly if you are led toward conclusions you don't want to reach.

A person can be partisan without being biased. That is why people sometimes arrive at conclusions in spite of their interests. Moreover, it is sometimes *because* people are partisan that they are most careful not to be biased. If a city activist is helping to map out a campaign to fight corrupt city leaders or capitalist developers, and really *cares* that the campaign is a success, then it would be most important that an analysis of city political forces on which the campaign is based is objective. The activist would take special pains to prevent bias from clouding his or her judgment.

Absolute and relative truth. Another rigid view of objectivity is that if people cannot know the entire truth about something all at once, then they cannot know *anything* at all about it. Some philosophers who presuppose this rigid view of objectivity conclude that since we obviously do not have this sort of "absolute knowledge" about things, therefore we do not know anything. Others advance the view that we can know everything about something but only relative to some point of view, for instance the point of view of our culture or our class or even just our own personal point of view. This theory, called "relativism," is still a sceptical one, because it maintains that you cannot tell whether any one point of view is objectively more true than any other point of view. It does not matter if you can have "absolute knowledge" *within* a point of view if you cannot know whether the point of view is itself objective. From a capitalist point of view, capitalism is unbeatable. From a socialist point of view it is doomed. What is important is which point of view is objectively correct about this crucial question.

In their theory of "absolute and relative truth" Marxists reject the alternative between absolute knowledge on the one hand and complete ignorance or relativism on the other. At one time people may know *part of* the truth about something. At a later time they will know more of the truth about it, and at a still later time, they know yet more. Newton knew more about the nature of physical bodies, space and time than the ancients. Einstein knew more than Newton, and physicists today have improved on Einstein's views. The fact that Einstein enlarged on and corrected Newton's theories does not mean that therefore Newton was entirely wrong, just that his views were limited.

Marxists say that while absolute knowledge about something is a goal to be striven for, our actual knowledge at any one time will always fall short of absolute knowledge. If we conduct our inquiries carefully, we will improve on the knowledge gained before. Similarly, our own beliefs will be corrected and improved by other people. Our views will be "relatively true" in a sense compatible with objectivity. Marxists do not see their own theories as exceptions to this. Marx and Engels corrected and improved their own views throughout their lifetimes. Later Marxists, such as Lenin in his work on imperialism, enlarged and corrected their theories more. Future Marxists will continue this process.

Objectivity and totalitarianism. One objection raised against Marxism is that belief in objectivity leads to "totalitarianism." It is said to do so because if somebody believes that they are objectively correct in holding a certain belief, they will feel justified in denying those who disagree with them a supposed basic human right to hold their own opinions.

In the first place, if respecting this right means that you should not attempt to change other people's opinions or that you should not try to prevent some opinions from being held at all, then it is questionable whether all people do have a right to their own opinions. If you knew someone with racist opinions and knew of a way to argue that person out of his or her racist views, shouldn't you try to do it? What is more, if you knew how to *prevent* people from coming to have racist opinions, should you not do this as well? The reason that people should be prevented from gaining or holding racist opinions is not just that these opinions are false, but that holding them leads people to do serious harm to other people. If

131

there had been no racist opinions in Hitler's Germany, nobody would have manned the gas chambers and the ovens.

In the second place, thinking that a belief you hold is objectively true does not make you prone to stifle other people's opinions, if you are convinced that in an atmosphere of free and open debate, the truth will out. (Racist opinions would be no exception to this were it not for the fact that they are almost never advanced in a spirit of objective debate, but are deliberately pushed in such a way as to encourage blind race hatred.) What is more, believing that it is possible to arrive at objectively true beliefs, you would welcome open discussion of varying opinions as a way of advancing your own knowledge.

If objectivism leads one to favour open debate and discussion, it is not so clear what anti-objectivism does. If you think that nobody can know what is true or false about things, then you *might* take the view that everybody should say what they think. But you might just as well follow a totalitarian line. First of all, if the anti-objectivist is right, then who is to say what is wrong with totalitarianism? Also, since life would be confusing with a variety of opinions each equally non-objective, you might think that what is needed is to commit yourself to one viewpoint and hold it dogmatically. One philosophical anti-objectivist, Mussolini, took just this attitude, and it is no secret how tolerant he was of other people's views.

CAPITALISM AND MATERIALISM

In its early days, capitalism favoured a qualified version of materialism. The materialist philosophy was necessary for the advancement of science, and hence of technology and profits. However, the materialist theories developed by pro-capitalist philosophers in the seventeenth and eighteenth centuries were quite simplistic and only went far enough to be of service to capitalism. They did not provide the basis for a fully humanistic view of the world. Also, capitalists have increasingly promoted the life style of *crass* materialism, since this creates more consumers for their often useless products.

Despite its early promotion of materialist theories, capitalism has by and large combated materialism. It is an obvious advantage to capitalists, as it has been to all oppressive ruling classes, to have working people look to an afterlife for rewards for their labours and to blame a divine power or their own "sinfulness" for their problems. It is an advantage to capitalists for people to think that things happen by chance or by individual efforts of will rather than to seek

132

out social laws and use them to change things. It is an advantage for capitalists to keep people in ignorance, and one way to do this is to promote the sceptical attitude that ignorance is the natural human condition.

On the other hand, the working class has everything to gain from the materialist philosophy of Marxism. Not the least advantage of this philosophy is that it contributes to revolutionary self-reliance. Once we understand that there are no other-worldly forces to come to our aid, and once we discover laws that show us how it is possible to change the world, then we cannot avoid the conclusion that it is we, ourselves, who must and can change it.

READINGS FOR CHAPTER ELEVEN

Reader in Marxist Philosophy, edited by H. Selsam & H. Martel (New York, New World Paperbacks, 1963, reprinted 1976). The selections in parts two, four, six, and seven include the most important passages from classic works on materialism.

F. Engels, *Socialism: Utopian and Scientific.* The introduction gives a Marxist materialist analysis of the class origins of English Protestantism.

V.I. Lenin, *Materialism and Empirio-Criticism* (in Vol. 14 of the *Collected Works*).

G. Plekhanov, *The Role of the Individual in History.* An early contemporary of Lenin, this Russian socialist wrote a defence of the Marxist view of determinism and the individual. It is available in pamphlet form in different editions and in any collection of Plekhanov's writings.

Mao Tse-tung, "On Practice." This short essay is a good defence of the Marxist view of objectivity. It can be found in any collection of Mao's writings, usually along with another essay, "On Contradiction," which contains some interesting suggestions regarding dialectics.

The passage quoted from Marx is in a December 28, 1846, letter to P.V. Annenkev, reprinted in Marx's *The Poverty of Philosophy* (Moscow, 1975, p. 167).

Chapter 12

DIALECTICS

One feature of everything around us is change. Individual humans change their views and their behaviour through the course of their lives. Societies change, as do plants and animals. Even things that do not appear to change, like lifeless objects and the solar system, change. A chair or a rock will eventually wear away or disintegrate. We now know that our solar system has not always existed and will someday cease to exist.

Marxist dialectics is the science of change in its most general aspects. It is part of a tradition in the history of philosophy that goes back to ancient times. Members of this tradition oppose another philosophical outlook that denies change. Some have actually tried to deny that *anything* changes. They say that change is an illusion. Others, like the ancient Greek philosophers Plato and Aristotle, have granted that some things change, but claim that the most important things do not. God, the soul, human nature and the structure of human societies have all been described as things that do not change.

Religious philosophers in the dialectical tradition, such as the influential nineteenth-century German philosopher, G.W.F. Hegel, have found it difficult to explain how God and the soul could change, since these things are thought to be unchanging by definition. This has not been a problem for Marxists, who, in their philosophical views, are atheists. The view that human nature or the structure of societies does not change is usually put forth to defend a politically conservative position. For instance, it is said that attempting revolutionary change is a waste of time, since humans are selfish by nature or since societies must always be divided into warring "interest groups." Marxists disagree for the reasons discussed in earlier chapters.

Dialectical philosophers differ among themselves on two questions: What changes? How do things change? On the first question, Marx and Engels differed from most previous advocates of dialectics and especially from Hegel. Hegel was an anti-materialist who believed that basically the world is non-material "spirit." Marxists maintain that what changes is the material world, including both its human and its non-human parts.

On the question of *how* things change, Marx and Engels were in agreement with Hegel, whose views they studied carefully. Dialectical philosophers have differed about the overall *pattern* of change. Some have even denied that there are any patterns and hold that change is a chaotic flux, with no laws or regularities. Hegel disagreed and set out to describe some very general characteristics of the way all things change. In this chapter I will summarize three of these characteristics as Marxists have taken them over from Hegel and interpreted in a materialistic way.

ENDLESS, SPIRALLING CHANGE

One characteristic of change is that it does not end. A seed grows into a plant which changes through its history until it dies and decays, changing into fertilizer for soil. This fertilized soil again changes as new plants draw on it for nutrition, and so on. The ideas, feelings and physical make-up and appearance of individual humans change throughout our lives. Unending change is also seen in the histories of animals, of planets and of everything else. In any process of change the thing that replaces what went before it, itself changes and is eventually replaced by something else.

It is the same with human societies. Once human beings had evolved from other forms of life, human society in Europe went through changes from primitive communism, to the slave-holding empires, to feudalism, to capitalism and now to socialism. At each transition in this history, as in any other process, some of the characteristics of what existed at an earlier stage were preserved in the stage that followed it, but in a radically new form.

The division of labour and use of machinery that began developing in the late Middle Ages were retained under capitalism but in the form of huge factories with complicated and massive machinery. The cooperative mode of work bred by the capitalist system continues into socialism, but stripped of capitalist exploitation, lack of planning and the other things that mark capitalist production. This will continue as socialism is transformed into communism. Some features will be retained, but in a stateless society there will be new features, and those that are retained will exist in a different way. This illustrates a central aspect of dialectics. As one thing replaces another thing, it typically retains features of the earlier thing, but in a new form. The entire process is thus a kind of spiral. (Marxists call this process of unending, spiralling change the law of the "negation of the negation.")

What about communism itself, will it also change? Most non-Marxist text books on Marxism claim that communism is seen by Marxists as an end to human change. Some of these texts claim that Marxists see communism as a perfect society where nothing would need to change. Others say that Marxists see history moving in a circle, with a return to early tribal communism.

No Marxist has ever claimed these things. They could not claim them and be consistent with dialectics. Advanced communism will be similar to early communism only in that it will not be class divided and there will be no state apparatus. There will also be *some* psychological similarities in that there will be a strong spirit of cooperation. Advanced communism will not be perfect, because there is no such thing as a perfect society. It will always be possible to extend human knowledge and experience. Moreover, despite our ability to change nature, we are still dependent on it, and nature is not perfectly suited to human well-being, as is evidenced by earthquakes and floods. How exactly will society continue to change under communism? This is not possible to say. It is hard enough to predict how we in Canada can best get rid of capitalism — which is two social orders from communism.

There is a useful Marxist distinction between change that is "antagonistic" and change that is "non-antagonistic." Antagonistic changes are hostile ones that involve destruction for one or more of the forces involved in change. Non-antagonistic change is not hostile and does not need to involve destruction. (An example of an antagonistic contradiction is that between the capitalist class and the working class. The contradiction between industrial and "white collar" or farmworkers united in struggle against capitalism and imperialism is non-antagonistic.) All we can say about changes under communism is that they will involve antagonistic relations between humans and nature, where humans will constantly have to be on guard against a potentially dangerous natural environment.

137

Communism will also change due to *non-antagonistic* relations among humans. People will develop and change out of mutually beneficial relations among themselves rather than as a result of class struggle.

RADICAL AND DETERMINED CHANGE

A radical change is one that involves a thoroughgoing alteration in the nature of what changes. Although there are some similarities between humans and other higher primates (like apes), humans are not just apes who, in addition to apelike qualities, have the ability to use tools and to talk. Humans are radically different from apes in that our whole mode of life and thought differs. Marxists maintain that socialism is not just capitalism with state-run factories. Marxists claim that there is a radical difference between the political, social and economic organization and development of socialist societies and of capitalist ones.

Many people assume that if something changes radically, then its change is not entirely determined by what went before, or, conversely, that if a change is entirely caused by what went before, then it cannot really be a radical one. For example, around the time that Darwin was advancing his theory of evolution, there were some who held that since humans are radically different from apes and other primates, they could not have evolved naturally from other animals — there had to be a "leap," which did not involve any natural causes. This view was popular with some people who wanted to reconcile evolution with religion. The radical differences between humans and other primates were explained by *supernatural* intervention in the evolutionary process. On the other hand, some determinists held (and still do hold) that if the origin of humans can be entirely explained by gradual changes in apelike primates, then there is no essential difference between humans and apes.

These views assume that something cannot be both radically new and also entirely caused by what has gone before, which is a central view of dialectics. In the example about evolution, for instance, Marxists follow Darwin in taking the dialectical perspective *both* that humans are radically different from other primates *and also* that the appearance of humans can be entirely explained by reference to the evolutionary process leading up to them. Gradual changes in the adaptation of some primates to their environment led to an animal radically different from the primates near the beginning of this evolutionary chain. Another example often given by

138

dialectical philosophers is that changes in the temperature of water at one point cause a radical change to ice. Ice is not just very cold water; it is thoroughly different. Yet water turning to ice can be entirely explained by the cumulative effect of changes in temperature on the water's molecular structure.

Marxists call this characteristic of change the dialectical law of "the transformation from quantity to quality and vice-versa." "Quantitative" changes in water's temperature lead to the "qualitative" change in its turning to ice. (I believe that Marx and Engels added "vice-versa" to their statement of the law to indicate that once a radical transformation has taken place, this in turn affects the quantitative things inherited from before. For instance, once humans had the use of tools and language, this began to have an effect on their still apelike posture and eating habits.)

The fact that change is both radical and determined is especially important for social revolutions. People who fail to understand it will be likely to attempt either reformist or foolhardy programs of action. If you think that all changes must be gradual, with no radical "leaps," then you will be apt to be overcautious and attempt to change things just by a series of reforms of capitalism. ("We have to maintain credibility.") If you think that radical change is not entirely determined by what goes before, you will strive to bring a revolution about without helping first to build a base for it. ("Revolution may not seem likely but wait until the workers see this poster.")

THE SOURCE OF CHANGE

To discover the specific causes of any one change, you must investigate the particular features of that change. Dialectics will not tell you what these features are. But if you think in a dialectical way, you will look for the primary source of something's changing *in* that thing itself. In this, dialectics differs from the outlook that things change only because of some outside influence — that if they were just left alone they would not change. One expression of this undialectical view is the "export of revolution" theory. If only it had not been for the subversive schemes of socialist countries, it is held, Vietnam would never have gone socialist. Latin Americans would be happy with their lot, so it is claimed, were it not for the influence of Cuba.

Marxists recognize that things always interact with their environment and with other things in very complicated ways, and that outside influences affect how something changes. For example, military aid from the socialist countries was very important for the people of Vietnam, and the example of Cuba has led many in Latin America to realize the advantages socialism would have for their own countries. But none of this means that things would stay the same without outside influence. Vietnam was locked in an anti-imperialist struggle, which would have led in a socialist direction regardless of contact with socialist countries, and the same is true for Latin America.

Marxists see the primary source of change *within* the things that change. Everything is composed of elements that work together or require one another and at the same time work against one another. As Marx and Engels put it, again following Hegel, things are "unities of opposites," or they contain "dialectical contradictions." In order to survive, a living organism must *acquire* energy (for instance, it must eat food) and it must also *expend* energy (for instance, to get food). Since living creatures expend energy to gain nutrition the two work together. But these elements also work against one another since the two activities never perfectly balance. Rather, the creature is either assimilating more than it expends (it grows), or it expends more than it assimilates (the final result is death).

In one respect this dialectical view is the opposite of an "equilibrium" view of things, such as the theory in social science called "functionalism." Functionalism maintains that the *natural* state of a society is to be in perfect equilibrium, where each part helps to keep the society just as it is without changing. Societies not in this "natural" state are either tending toward it or simply disintegrating. For dialectics this fails to see that in addition to supporting one another, the parts of a society also work against one another. We have seen a Marxist application of this unity of opposites in the theory of the contradiction between the forces and the relations of production within a society. The relations of production under capitalism *require* that the forces of production include a well-organized, low paid work force, but this work force becomes capitalism's "grave digger." To survive as a social system, capitalism requires something that finally becomes incompatible with its continued existence. The result is that capitalism cannot survive.

Lenin referred to the law of the unity of opposites as the most important law of dialectics. A major aim of scientific socialism is to identify dialectical contradictions within particular societies at different stages of their histories. I will look at some more examples later. But first, two common objections to Marxist dialectics should be met.

Some object to Marxist dialectics on the grounds that the same laws could not apply both to human societies and to nature. One reason sometimes given for this objection is that Marxists obscure the essential differences between humans and nature by saying that they share some characteristics in common. This is a mistake. Both plants and planets are known to obey the law of gravity, but this does not mean that botanists and astronomers fail to see the distinctive differences between them. In fact, sometimes by seeing general shared characteristics, important differences become clear. For instance, looking for the dialectical contradictions in both the animal world and in human history puts into sharper focus that which is *unique* to human change — the dialectics of social labour with tools.

Other reasons for resisting the view that both human history and nature share general dialectical characteristics are based on some aspect of anti-materialism as discussed in the last chapter. *Anti-determinists* think it opposes human creativity to think of people as acting in accord with natural laws. *Anti-objectivists* are only prepared to admit a sort of "dialectics" compatible with their relativism. (Some anti-materialists who would like to consider themselves Marxist say that their objections relate only to Engels, and that Marx thought dialectics does not apply to nature. For reasons given in the appendix, I believe this view is mistaken.)

DIALECTICS AND BLUEPRINTS

It is charged by some that the Marxist theory of dialectics is an attempt to impose a preconceived scheme on things in the hopes of finding simple solutions to complicated problems. In fact, dialectics is not a preconceived scheme, but a theory evolved by philosophers over several centuries and tested in everyday experience and science. Like any other theory it is subject to change. No Marxist can expect that 100 years from now the theory will not have been considerably changed.

Dialectics is very general. Something that does not appear to be changing *is* nonetheless changing partly because of internal features that may not be obvious at first sight. But dialectics in general will not tell *what* those features are. For this, it is necessary to examine things themselves in their particular details. Dialectics indicates that a radical change in something is caused by what preceded it, but the general theory of dialectics won't unearth those causes. Again, it is necessary to study the history of particular things. In this respect, dialectics is like other general scientific theories. Knowing the law of gravity will not tell you what the exact gravitational attractions are among specific bodies. For this you need to examine those bodies themselves. Dialectics is useful because it alerts one to the fact that things are all changing and the complexities of change.

The view that radical changes are determined alerts one to the need to move carefully to help build a base for social change. At the same time, it alerts one to the need to work toward *radical* change and to move resolutely and quickly when the time comes.

The dialectical view that there is no end to change warns against seeing any process of change as reaching an end. Anybody who thinks that getting rid of capitalism will forever end problems in society or the need for further social change is not thinking dialectically and will be in for a rude shock when confronted with the problems of building socialism. Understanding the "spiral" character of this change guards one against both a wholesale rejection of what went before and assuming that transformations involve a simple rearrangement of things. Thus while many things developed in capitalism (for instance, public services or educational institutions, not to mention capitalist developed technology) can be incorporated by socialism, they cannot be taken over just as they are, but must be reconstructed to fit in with a planned, worker-oriented society.

The dialectical theory of the unity of opposites cautions one against overlooking how at the same time things work together and work against each other. The practical benefits of this perspective can be seen by taking two examples: reform and revolution, and nationalism and internationalism.

REFORM AND REVOLUTION

A "reform" activity, demand or movement is one that aims to defend people against some bad effect of capitalism or to make things better without toppling the capitalist system itself. The aim of a reform movement is to make changes that are possible *within* the capitalist system, even if some capitalists may not like the changes. The trade union movement is a reform movement. It aims for better wages and working conditions within the present capitalist system. Organizations that aim to combat racism and sexism advance reform demands, as do peace groups and organizations struggling for community or municipal reforms.

A "revolutionary" movement or activity, on the other hand, is one that aims to end the social system of capitalism altogether and replace it with socialism. Revolutionary goals cannot be achieved

142

within the present system, because the central revolutionary goal is to do away with this system. Obviously, there is an important difference between a reform goal and a revolutionary one. At the same time movements for revolutionary change have always grown out of reform movements. In the history of people's struggles, reform activities and ideas and revolutionary ones are a dialectical unity of opposites. To show what this means, I will indicate the dangers involved in undialectical approaches to reform and revolution.

The opposition of reform and revolution. The main effect of failing to see the difference between reform and revolution is to adopt the *reformist* approach discussed in chapter six. Since on a very general level revolution and reform favour the same thing — a better world — it is therefore thought that all one needs to do is to keep reforming the present system until we reach that world. But the present system, which is based on the drive for private profit, simply is not structured to ensure human happiness and progress.

Capitalists and capitalist-dominated governments can be forced to allow some changes for the better, but they will do everything in their power to prevent society from being reorganized in the interests of working people. They are not prepared to allow working people to determine what is produced, how it is produced, what wages will be, who is to control the state and so on. To gain these things a revolution is necessary, which requires a consciously organized effort of working people to replace the system of capitalism altogether. The result of reformist thinking is not only to set back revolution, but also to inhibit reform. Capitalists do not like to give up anything that eats into profits. If a reformist does not want to make any demands that might make capitalists angry, he will find the demands he can push for are very small ones.

Another effect of failing to understand the crucial difference between reform and revolution is trying to convert reform organizations and demands into revolutionary ones. I have been in many peace groups and organizations for university reform. In nearly every one of them, people have taken the position that this group is in fact the vanguard of the revolution. This situation is not unique to groups I happen to have been in, but exists in the women's and civil rights movements, in community or high school organizations, and in the trade union movement. While most participants think that the aim of these groups is, for example, to stop Canadian arms sales, or to win government support for social services, or to combat racial or ethnic discrimination, others think that the aim is to bring about the socialist revolution.

This viewpoint results from the realization that capitalism is the cause of what reform groups combat, but a failure to realize that there is a difference between struggling for particular reforms and struggling to topple the capitalist system. Some assume that since what they are combating is caused by capitalism, any measure against it is a revolutionary one. Others assume that no reform can be made unless the reform group succeeds in ending the system.

When these undialectical ways of thinking prevail, reforms that could be won are not. Either they are not struggled for at all, or they are presented in such a way that people in the group feel they have to be prepared to support social revolution as well. Given the level of revolutionary consciousness in North America today, this approach guarantees little support.

The unity of reform and revolution. I have noted how reformist thinking inhibits reform. A revolutionary perspective has the opposite effect. By relating reform demands to class struggle, a revolutionary view of things identifies the main enemy to fight and cautions against trying to win favour with the "Establishment." Thus maximum success in reform requires a revolutionary viewpoint. It is no less true that successful revolution requires successful reform.

Look at the forces for and against revolution. On the one side, working people constitute the overwhelming majority of the population, and they have the valuable cooperative and disciplined skills and attitudes necessary for revolution. On the other side, the capitalists have the power of the state. They are experts at dividing people, and while, relatively speaking, *they* know the score, they strive to keep working people in ignorance. In particular they strive to keep people ignorant of the causes of problems in society, and they strive to convince people that they are not strong enough to change things.

Success in revolution depends on people identifying their main enemy and gaining the confidence and unity necessary to overcome the capitalist state. Where will these skills come from? They are not going to come out of thin air, but out of practical activity. It is in *reform* activity, in working with other people to bring about a particular reform, that people learn the main source of problems and that it is possible, through concerted and united activity, to combat the capitalist system and force capitalists to give up some things to the people. Once this lesson is learned it is not that great a step to revolutionary activity — that is, to activity that strives to take *everything* from the capitalist by ending the system of capitalism altogether.

Some people who want socialism see reform work as detracting from revolution, by watering down revolutionary zeal and misleading people into thinking that capitalism can solve all its problems. This viewpoint might have some validity if revolution were already on the agenda. If the working class in a society had the determination and ability to topple capitalism, it would be wrong to push for more limited demands. At that point, such demands would be rejected by revolutionary workers themselves. Revolutions require the broadest support, and it is only in reform work that this support can be formed.

Undialectical thinking is not, unfortunately, confined only to "revolutionaries" who shun reform work. It is also found on the part of many who work in reform movements despite their failure to understand the unity of reform and revolution. Such people sometimes do this as an attempt to convert the reform movements into revolutionary ones. This almost always backfires, since it is usually just a matter of time before they are kicked out of the reform movement or everyone else quits so they can preach the sins of reform alone, to one another.

Others go into reform movements *hoping* the movements will fail. The strategy is to join or create a reform movement, push demands that are likely not to be won, and then recruit for the revolution those who are "educated" to the futility of reform. To my knowledge, this strategy has never succeeded in doing anything but discouraging people about the possibility of making any gains at all. It has fed the capitalist-inspired line that the people are not strong enough to do anything to better their lot. Success is a much better teacher than failure.

It is perhaps more important to have a dialectical understanding of the relation between reform and revolution than of anything else. The history of people's movements has been the history of the interplay between reform demands and perspectives and revolutionary ones. In each case the success or failure, both of reform and of revolution, has depended in part on the ability of people involved to understand these processes dialectically.

NATIONALISM AND INTERNATIONALISM

The question of nationalism is a very important one for Canadians. In addition to the original native nationalities that have survived, there are the French-speaking and English-speaking peoples who constitute the majority of the two nations of Confederation. There are also a number of other important groups — Ukrainian, Chinese, Italian, Greek and so on — which, though they do not form geographically contained nations in the country, have retained a good part of the identity of their ethnic origins.

Concern about one's nation has both served working-class interests and played against those interests. When nationalism, as a one-sided attitude hostile to other nations, is used to divide working people or to gain support for capitalist governments in the supposed interests of "the nation," it sets back working people's struggles. During World War I, nationalistic sentiments were used to turn working people against one another to fight for warring capitalist states rather than to unite against world capitalism. Capitalist states use nationalism in their campaigns against socialist countries and movements. They also use nationalistic loyalties to justify economic "sacrifices" they claim working people have to make in the "national interest."

A national orientation can also be progressive. In many countries the struggle for national self-determination against imperialists is an important democratic struggle that serves to unite people in campaigns for liberation. A progressive national perspective emphasizes the development and protection of a nation's cultural and economic potentials insofar as these grow out of and serve to enrich the working people of that nation.

Internationalism, too, is an attitude with more than one side. Marxists have always maintained that working-class success in struggles against capitalism require "proletarian internationalism," that is, the greatest possible unity among workers of all nations. As the humanistic attitude that people in different nations should view one another as members of a human community and avoid war and national chauvinism, internationalism is also obviously progressive. But as an attitude on the part of capitalists that the whole world should be a vast resource of cheap labour and captive markets, "internationalism" is quite another thing.

The relation between nationalism and internationalism is surrounded with almost as much confused and undialectical thinking as reform and revolution. In fact, the two topics are closely related, since campaigns for national self-determination are reform movements that quickly educate people to a revolutionary perspective, because they immediately bring them up against the usually anti-national force of imperialism. At the same time imperialists

146

attempt to use nationalism at home to enlist support for wars against national liberation abroad. I will conclude this chapter by making some comments about how nationalism and internationalism are a unity of opposites.

World revolution and Canada. As in the case of reform and revolution, people who think undialectically about nationalism and internationalism either fail to see tensions between these things or they fail to see how they work together. For example, some socialists seem to think there must be a single world pattern for achieving and building socialism. Sometimes a particular socialist country is picked as the model everybody should follow (which country depends on who is doing the picking). Other times, an abstract idea of what socialism should be like everywhere is the standard.

This approach fails to see the importance of national differences. How socialism is achieved and built in Canada will depend on the particular political, economic and cultural circumstances of the nations and the different nationalities that make it up. It could only harm the cause of building socialism here to insist on some detailed scheme supposedly valid internationally.

On the other side, there are those who fail to see the unity of working classes of all nations. They take a "Canada should go it alone" view. This is also a dangerous perspective. As recent struggles for national liberation have taught us, international support is badly needed. Political, moral, and where possible economic and military support have been important factors in the struggles in Vietnam and other parts of Asia, Africa and Latin America. The perspective also makes it more difficult to see similarities and differences between Canada and present-day socialist countries and to learn from their mistakes and their successes. Finally, this point of view overlooks the fact that there are obviously some elements of a socialist transformation that apply in all countries (for instance, the need to form alliances and to guard against counter-revolution).

When we gain socialism in Canada we will need all the support we can get. If the U.S. is still capitalist, we will need to form economic and even military alliances with other socialist countries to resist imperialist blackmail and attempts to sabotage us. We will need political support from people all over the world. It will not be to our advantage at all to take a go-it-alone attitude. Capitalists do not hesitate to ignore national boundaries, and sometimes try to obliterate them altogether. In attempting to get rid of capitalism here, the working class of Canada should not deny itself revolutionary working-class support from any place in the world.

Canada and the U.S. Similar examples of undialectical thinking can be seen in relation to Canada and the United States. On both the left and the right there are those who take a "continentalist" approach and oppose any demands for political, economic or cultural autonomy from the U.S. The right-wing version tries to maintain that Canada benefits from its relation to the U.S. Those on the left argue that demands for Canadian national self-determination detract from working-class struggle. There are others — again to be found both on the left and on the right — who see practically anything that is of Canadian origin as good and anything coming from the U.S. as bad.

The continentalist approach ignores some important differences between Canada and the U.S. Continentalists who think we benefit from being politically and economically dominated by the largest imperialist power in the world had better take a look at its effects on the lives of Canadian workers. Because of U.S. domination of the economy, prices here are higher than in the U.S. and in general wages are lower. What is more, branch plants of U.S.-owned industries lay people off or close down in response to the needs of the U.S. economy. Canadians are forced to help subsidize U.S. capitalists who receive various tax and other benefits from the Canadian government.

Left continentalists fail to see that demands for national self-determination are in part democratic demands. To the extent that they are won, they put working people in a better position to determine for themselves how they are to live and work. In our case, the struggle for self-determination and the struggle against capitalism cannot easily be separated since the dominant capitalist control of Canadian working people is U.S. centred. To argue that the Canadian working class can make no gains until the U.S. working class does is also a mistake. In some respects the Canadian working class is more advanced than the U.S. one. Since the U.S. lacks a large third party with working-class support, workers there have less political experience than Canadian workers. And thanks to U.S. domination of the Canadian economy, Canadian workers have a better understanding of imperialism.

Many anti-continentalists also take a one-sided and undialectical view. It is true that Canada is a victim of imperialism, but it is still a capitalist country with its own capitalist interests. In a small way relative to the U.S., Canada is also an imperialist force, as in Brazil and Jamaica, for example. Canadian capitalists who are themselves imperialists are quite content to allow U.S. capitalism to dominate our country as long as their own schemes are not interfered with. Domestically, Canadian capitalists are no less motivated by greed for profit than are capitalists any place else in the world.

Trade union decisions affecting Canadian unionists should be made by Canadians. But this does not mean that therefore any Canadian union is automatically one that best serves Canadian working people's interests and any international union is bad for Canadian workers. A progressive international union that includes autonomy for its Canadian chapter may be preferable to a reactionary all-Canadian union.

Rigid "either . . . or" thinking is not dialectical. You cannot decide what is the best thing to do by appealing to a simple rule like: "If it is in the interests of the nation it is good" or "If it is in the interests of just one nation it is bad." Rather, things must be evaluated in their concrete settings, taking account of the always changing balance of class forces both within and across national boundaries.

Quebec. Canada has been one state made up of two nations. Hence we have had a "national question" right within Canada itself. The French-speaking majority in Quebec have long sought to be masters in their own house. In spite of the platitudes expressed by the federal government, it, the capitalist class in Canada and most of the English language press have taken the line that Quebec is just one province among others and has no unique rights in matters such as determining its own economy or insisting on the use of its own language, much less in determining whether it remains in Confederation.

This line is, in the first place, self serving, since English-Canadian capitalism profits from the arrangement. Relatively speaking wages have been low in Quebec while prices have remained high. The position fails to recognize that Quebec has a unique existence. It is not just one province among others, but it is an entire nation covering a larger geographic area than most European countries, with a language and culture of its own, and potentially forming a viable independent economic and political unit. What is more, Quebec has always been regarded by the Anglophone ruling class of Canada as a conquered and inferior nation and thus fair game for economic plunder.

149

The view opposing Quebec's national self-determination is put forth in the name of "Canadian unity," but in fact it is a great source of *disunity*. It creates and feeds intense national chauvinism and language bigotry against French-speaking Canadians, both inside and outside Quebec. It has created a situation where more and more Quebeckers see no solution but to opt out of Confederation. In Quebec and in English-speaking Canada as well, it has also fed the attitude on the part of some that separation is the solution to all the problems of the people of Quebec.

This attitude is also undialectical. Even if separation were to be better than Confederation on new terms, it is no cure-all. It makes a difference whether a new Quebec state would be advantageous to the *working class* in Quebec. Separation itself does not guarantee this. For that matter, there is no guarantee that federation on new terms would be in the interests of Quebec workers. Everything depends on the terms.

National and international feelings should no more be set against one another in the case of Quebec than in any other case. Whether the people of Quebec choose to remain in Confederation or to leave it, the right to national self-determination of the Quebec working class should be supported by the working class in English-speaking Canada. For the working class in Quebec or anyplace else in Canada to take control of its own conditions of life and work, it will finally have to take that control away from capitalists. This requires the greatest amount of internal working-class support. At the same time, achieving this *unity* requires that Canadian working people respect one another's national *differences*.

READINGS FOR CHAPTER TWELVE

Reader in Marxist Philosophy, edited by H. Selsam & H. Martel (New York, New World Paperbacks, 1963, reprinted 1976). Part Three is devoted to dialectics.

F. Engels, *Anti-Dühring*. This book, available in both New World Paperbacks and in a Soviet edition, contains the first attempt by a Marxist to discuss the basic views of Marxist dialectics in a more or less systematic way. Part I is devoted to dialectics.

F. Engels, *Socialism: Utopian and Scientific*. Part II summarizes some of the important views of dialectics.

F. Engels, *Dialectics of Nature* (New York, New World Paperbacks, 1963). Some notes by Engels in which he applies dialectical materialism to some developments in the history of the natural sciences. This edition has some useful notes and an introduction by the English Marxist scientist, J.B.S. Haldane.

F. Engels, *Ludwig Feuerbach and the End of Classic German Philosophy*. Here Engels summarizes the development both of Marxist dialectics and materialism, contrasting Marxism to other approaches in philosophy.

V.I. Lenin, *Philosophical Notebooks* (Volume 38 of the *Collected Works*). Notes Lenin made on some famous philosophers, mainly Aristotle and Hegel.

V.I. Lenin, *What is to Be Done?* and *Left-Wing Communism, An Infantile Disorder* (in Volumes 5 and 31 respectively of the *Collected Works*). In these works Lenin criticizes reformists and anti-reform leftists.

V.I. Lenin, *The Right of Nations to Self-Determination* (in Volume 20 of the *Collected Works*). A summary of Lenin's views on the "national question" and on the relation between socialism and the struggle for national self-determination.

J. Stalin, *The National Question and Leninism* (in Vol. 11 of *Joseph Stalin Collected Works*, Moscow 1954). Despite some of the things which he *did* regarding national rights within the Soviet Union, Stalin wrote a classic Marxist work on the national question.

151

Chapter 13

MARXISM AND CANADA

A common charge of anti-Marxists in Canada is that while Marxism may apply in some other countries, or may have applied to some parts of the world at an earlier time, it is not applicable to present-day Canada. This charge is not only made by Canadian anti-Marxists. It is also made by anti-Marxists in practically every country in the capitalist world, each claiming that his country is an exception to Marxist principles. Of course, the charge is an attempt to discredit Marxism as a scientifically correct analysis of Canadian society. But it is more than that. It is part and parcel of a pro-capitalist propaganda campaign designed to make working people think of socialism as something completely foreign to them and as an intrusion on the "normal" Canadian way of life. During the cold war, the campaign was especially intense but even now its advocates continue to picture Communists as subversives, socialist ideas as a kind of disease and socialist countries as other planets.

The obvious aim of this propaganda is to make the idea of socialism in Canada unthinkable to the working class. But since more and more working people are thinking of a socialist Canada, the campaign has obviously failed. Whatever the intentions of various NDP leaders may be, many of the people who belong to and vote for the NDP do so in the belief that they are voting for socialism. The Communist Party of Canada is growing. Many of those in Quebec who are struggling for their national rights regard it as equally a struggle for socialism. Organizations such as trade unions, community groups, the women's movement, farmers' organizations, organizations of native peoples, immigrant groups and others all include growing numbers who have come to see the necessity of socialism in Canada.

Along with this growing awareness, there has been an increasing interest in Marxism. Student pressure has forced Marxist studies into the high schools, community colleges and universities. Marxist literature can now be found in almost any bookstore. All over the country there are study groups and lectures devoted to Marxism. Nor is this interest new. In the 1930s and the 1940s, before the cold war, Marxist study was pursued on a scale we have only recently regained and started to surpass. Even in the last century, when Marx and Engels were still alive, there was interest in their views on the part of Canadian working people's movements and progressive forces. In fact, in 1872, while Marx was still writing *Capital*, an excerpt from Volume I of that work was published in *The Ontario Worker*, the first labour paper in Canada.

To prove that Marxism does not apply to Canada somebody would have to show either that the Canadian working class does not need socialism or that Marxism would not help them. The reason that anti-Marxists seldom try to give these proofs is that they cannot give them.

It is hard to argue that a capitalist Canada meets the needs of working people when, according to government statistics, 25 per cent of our people live below the poverty line and nearly ten per cent are unemployed. (In some parts of the country, such as the North, Newfoundland and the Maritimes, the figures are even higher.) Less than 25 million Canadians live in the second largest country in the world, rich in natural resources. Yet we suffer from high prices for energy, food and building materials. Is this how capitalism serves our interests? Have Canadian capitalists and the pro-capitalist governments met our needs by their complicity in the domination of the country's economy by U.S. based monopolies?

Canada is said to be a "democracy" where there are free elections to a Parliament which represents the people. Why is it then that our elected government officials (predominately either Tories or Liberals) take turns enacting legislation that favours big business against the interests of the working person? Why do they break the promises they make in multi-million dollar election campaigns so fast it is hard to keep track?

Canada is said to be a land of equal opportunity for all. But what equal opportunity exists for the native peoples of this country, whose treaty rights are regularly broken and whose traditional means of livelihood are denied? What equal opportunity exists for

154

the Black person or the recent immigrant who is less likely to get a good education or a high-paying job than a native-born white Canadian?

What equal opportunity is there for women, who are paid less for doing the same sort of work as men? Indeed, what equal opportunity exists in a country where money talks and where there are a few millionaires (most born into their money) while the average Canadian has to pay between a quarter and a half of his or her income for rent or mortgage payments and has to think twice before taking off even a single day's work? Attending all these special problems there is a deep sense of insecurity about the future, over which Canadians have little control as long as our society is dominated by the moneyed few.

To overcome these and other problems, Canadian working men and women need to run the country in their own interests. That is, as more and more are coming to realize, they need socialism.

MARXISM, YESTERDAY AND TODAY

People who say that Marxism does not apply to Canadian conditions sometimes say that this is because present-day Canada is different from nineteenth-century Germany or England, and sometimes they say that it is because Canada is different from the Russia of 1917 or the China of 1949. True enough. But this does not mean that Marxism does not apply to us. Canada shares some of the very general social conditions that led to the Russian and Chinese revolutions among many others.

Canada is a class-divided society in which an ever-growing number of people are being driven into the working class, or out of work altogether. We suffer from all the problems typically caused by capitalism such as chronic unemployment and inflation. Capitalists, both home grown and foreign, squeeze profits out of the labour of working people, create bad working conditions, lay waste to our resources and environment, destroy people's cultures, strive to turn working people against each other, and in short do all the things capitalists around the world have always done.

Meanwhile, the Canadian working class has responded like all other working classes. Initially it formed trade unions to fight against the capitalists' economic assault on working people. Political parties based in the working class were formed. More and more working people are seeing the need to forge alliances with other segments of Canadian society that are squeezed by big business and to challenge the political domination of Canada by pro-capitalist governments. All these sorts of things were predicted by Marx and Engels. They result from common features of all capitalist societies.

On the other hand, these similarities do not mean that the Marxism of a century ago provides a detailed analysis of contemporary Canada or a specific plan of action. Marx and Engels developed a general theory of class society, not a scheme that can be applied in just the same way everywhere. In this respect Marxism is like any scientific theory. The general laws of physics apply both to the earth and to the moon, but naturally not in precisely the same ways. When Marx himself used his theory to explain different things (for instance, the totalitarian coup in France in 1852 and the U.S. Civil War) he did not give the same explanation, but took account of the specific differences in the events he was analyzing.

Marx had no trouble applying a single theory to different situations while recognizing their differences. The same thing is possible in the application and development of Marxist theory to solve the problems involved in gaining socialism in different countries. The most basic theoretical views of Marxism are general enough to apply to all countries in the modern world. But they do not provide people with what Marxists call the "strategy and tactics" to follow in a particular country at a particular time. For this you need to study the country itself and further develop the theory.

In applying Marxism to his own society Lenin broadened the theory as he worked out the strategy of forging a main alliance between industrial workers and the peasantry. Obviously, it would be foolish to adopt this strategy in Canada, since we do not have a large peasantry. The working class here needs to form an alliance with all those other sectors of Canadian society whose interests are opposed to the monopolies: professionals, farmers, intellectuals, small businessmen and others. There is no blueprint in Marxist theory that tells how to do this.

Of course there are some important similarities between Canada and other countries, and we must learn from those also striving to forge such alliances. But there are other features that make Canada unique. Canada's geography and regional differences, the structure of its levels of government, the relation of Quebec to English Canada, the relation of domestic to foreign-based capitalism making Canada both a victim of imperialism and a mini-imperialist, the blend of development and underdevelopment — all these features and more make for important differences between Canada and other countries. We in Canada need the general theory of Marxism to help us understand the nature, development and interrelations of these specific features. We need the theory of Marxism to follow an effective road to socialism in Canada.

READINGS FOR CHAPTER THIRTEEN

Stanley Ryerson, *The Founding of Canada* and *Unequal Union*. These two books by a Canadian Marxist historian apply Marxist theory to the history of Canada. Both books are published by Progress Publishers, Toronto (reprinted in 1975); the first goes up to 1815, the second to 1873.

F. &. L. Park, *Anatomy of Big Business* (Toronto, Progress Publishers, 1962, reprinted, James Lewis and Samuel, 1973). Though now somewhat dated, this book contains some useful facts about the corporate structure of Canada.

W. Clement, *The Canadian Corporate Elite* (Toronto, Carleton Library Original, 1975). Although Clement does not always use Marxist categories, this book contains many statistics that all go to verify the applicability of Marxism to Canada.

The Road to Socialism in Canada (Toronto, Progress Publishers.) The program of the Communist Party of Canada.

Appendix

MARX, ENGELS, LENIN

Karl Marx was born in 1818 in the city of Trier. His father was a lawyer of German Jewish origins, who, like a number of Jewish professionals of his time, made a gesture of accepting Protestantism. Marx studied law and philosophy, writing a doctoral thesis on the ancient Greek thinkers, Democritus and Epicurus. Like all students of philosophy then he was acquainted with the works of Hegel. Some maintain that in his early years Marx was a Hegelian but he abandoned this philosophy as he grew older. In fact, what Marx says about Hegel shows that in his younger years, he was more critical of Hegel than in his later ones. *Capital,* the first volume of which appeared in 1867, contains several approving references to Hegel and includes many Hegelian ideas and phrases.

One side of Hegel that Marx never liked was his anti-materialist, religious viewpoint and the support his philosophy provided for a conservative political establishment. Even as a youth Marx favoured a materialist approach to the world and was not one to accept conventional wisdom. At the age of seventeen he wrote a school composition on the subject of choosing a profession in which he said:

> We cannot always take up the profession for which we feel ourselves suited; our relations in society have begun to crystallize more or less before we are in a position to determine them.

If this seems commonplace to us now, it is partly because of the work Marx himself did to show how people lack control over their lives and work under capitalism.

In 1842 Marx became editor of a left-leaning newspaper in

159

Cologne and an important member of a community of left intellectuals there. At that time he was greatly influenced by a famous atheist of the time, Ludwig Feuerbach. Feuerbach put forth the theory that religion was a product of human "alienation" whereby human qualities become projected onto an imaginary divinity. Marx developed the theory of alienation in a more concrete way, writing some manuscripts in 1844, which discussed people's "alienation" from the products and the process of their daily work and from nature and one another.

At this time Marx did not yet have a very clear idea about the nature of economic classes and class antagonisms. Rather, he was in the process of evolving the theory of class struggle. In this task he was joined by Frederick Engels.

Engels was born into a well-to-do family in the Prussian town of Barmen in 1820. Engels worked for his manufacturer father and pursued scientific and philosophical studies on his own. He also spent some time in the military which, along with studies he pursued later, made Engels quite knowledgeable about military science.

In 1842 Engels moved to Manchester in England to work for a firm in which his father had interests. By this time his views had become anti-capitalist and he researched the conditions of life and work of the English working class. The result was a book on the subject published in 1845. During this time also Engels contributed material to the left publication Marx was associated with. In 1844 they met in Paris and found that they were thinking along the same lines. From then on Marx and Engels worked very closely together. In 1845 and 1846 they co-authored two books (*The Holy Family* and *The German Ideology*) in which they criticized the left intellectuals of their circle and, in the second of these books, Feuerbach, for failing to think scientifically or to see the importance of class struggle and the working class.

Marx and Engels were key figures in organizing the Communist League, an organization of Communist workers and intellectuals from across Europe, for which they drafted the *Communist Manifesto* in 1848. In 1849 Marx was exiled from Germany to Paris and then to England. He continued political work in London, and in 1864 he and Engels were again central in organizing the International Workingmen's Association (the first working-class International).

Until his death in 1883, Marx's main work in England was devoted to economic research, which led to his major book. Volume One of *Capital* appeared before his death. Times were always hard for him and his family. His wife died two years before him, and several children died in childhood. He left three daughters.

Engels lived in England and pursued research into politics, history, anthropology and the history of materialism in natural science. After Marx's death he completed *Capital*. Engels helped to found the Second International in 1889, and he acted as a sort of consultant for revolutionaries who came to England from all over Europe. He was well suited for this role not only because of his political knowledge and experience, but also because he was fluent in several languages, speaking 12 well and able to read many more. Engels died at the age of 75 in 1895.

V.I. Lenin was born into a middle-class family in the Russian town of Simbirsk (now Ulyanovsk) in 1870. He completed his law studies, but not before being arrested for activities as a student radical. In 1893 Lenin moved to St. Petersburg where he organized a socialist group and taught Marxism. For this activity he was again arrested, sent to Siberia and eventually forced to move to western Europe where he organized and wrote. In 1903 Lenin was a key figure in the founding of the Bolshevik Party which played an important role in the anti-Czarist bourgeois revolution of 1905 and the leading role in the socialist revolution of 1917. He was the important leader of the new Soviet state until his death in 1924.

Throughout his active political life, Lenin continually did research and wrote books and pamphlets on politics, economics and philosophy. Even the most abstract of this research was not done in a political vacuum. For instance, in 1908 Lenin wrote a criticism of a school of philosophers called "Empirio-Critics" (or Positivists) which included an analysis of philosophical trends from the eighteenth century. The practical, political importance of this task was to counteract some intellectuals in the Russian socialist movement, including some Bolsheviks, who were using the theories of the Empirio-Critics to justify an attack on the revolutionary mainstream of the Bolshevik Party.

WILL THE REAL MARX PLEASE STAND UP?

Until recently anti-communists have attacked all the leading theoretical founders of Marxism. As Marxism has become more popular, however, some have started to claim that Marxism is all right as long as it is stripped of its scientific and revolutionary dimensions. This is a neat trick, since Marxism *is* a science of revolution. The attempt to de-Marxize Marxism is done by claiming that many important views of Marx are opposed to those of Engels and Lenin. So-called Marx scholars pore over the texts taking a word here, a phrase there and interpreting them in strange ways to make their case.

Sometimes the very early writings of Marx are produced as evidence. This proves little, since in his works before about 1845 Marx was just starting to form his basic ideas. Even so, I believe that in the early works Marx does not express the anti-scientific and anti-revolutionary views attributed to him. Perhaps the Marx "scholars" seize on these works because they are relatively obscure, mostly composed of notes Marx wrote to himself, so it is easier to interpret them in different ways.

The two main points on which Marx is said to differ from Engels are what I called "determinism" and "objectivism" in chapter eleven. Unlike Engels, Marx is held to be an anti-determinist and an anti-objectivist. There are several things to be said about this interpretation of Marx.

(1) If there *were* differences between Marx and Engels on these two points, then Engels would be correct and Marx mistaken, so the mistaken views should not be retained in the theory of Marxism. If someone found this upsetting they could change the name of the theory to "Engelsianism" or something.

(2) In fact, it is only by making strained interpretations of a few passages taken out of context that Marx can be made out to oppose determinism and objectivism. Straightforward interpretations of most of his writings show that he agrees with Engels. Regarding objectivity, Marx once praised the economist, David Ricardo, for sometimes coming to "scientifically honest" and "scientifically necessary" conclusions, even though the conclusions were at variance with the class position favoured by Ricardo. In a preface to *Capital* Marx held that some social conditions are favourable for objective inquiry, others are not. These are not the sorts of remarks that are made by someone who thinks that objectivity is either undesirable or impossible.

In *Capital* Marx wrote:

Intrinsically, it is not a question of the higher or lower degree of development of the social antagonisms that result from the natural laws of capitalist production. It is a question of these laws themselves, of these tendencies working with iron necessity toward inevitable results.

Or in the *German Ideology,* in a marginal note in Marx's handwriting, it is said:

Men have history because they must *produce* their life and

because they must produce it moreover in a *certain* way; this is determined by their physical organization; their consciousness is determined in just the same way.

Are these the sort of things an anti-determinist would write?

(3) There was a division of labour between Marx and Engels in which Engels did most of the philosophical writing. Marx and Engels corresponded about all their work. We have the bulk of their correspondence and find in it only praise by Marx for Engels' philosophical views. Engels' main philosophical work is *Anti-Dühring*. In this book his views on determinism and objectivity are clearly set forth, as is his view that dialectics applies both to humans and to nature. Engels wrote this book on the urging of Marx, and a section on the dialectics of nature was written to defend some comments by Marx in *Capital*. Marx went over the entire manuscript and contributed a chapter himself (chapter X of part II). Why, if Marx disagreed on some of the most fundamental things Engels held, did he not say so?

(4) The view that Marx and Engels differed is often linked to a theory that Marx was more concerned with "practice" than Engels. This viewpoint probably comes from the mistaken opinion discussed in chapter eleven that all determinists are fatalists. In any case, it is a mistake to oppose science and practice. Marx was indeed opposed to constructing theories for their own sake. But so was Engels. Marx and Engels were both concerned to discover *causes* in society as it really, *objectively* is, precisely in order to guide effective practice.

Marx is said to differ from Lenin on two crucial points also — one philosophical and one political. The philosophical point comes again to the question of objectivity. Lenin described the Marxist theory of truth as a theory of "reflection" or a "copy" theory. Our ideas are true, he wrote, if they "reflect" or "copy" reality. This is said to prove that Lenin held the simplistic view that our ideas are like little mirrors or drawings that perfectly reproduce what is outside us. Since Lenin frequently talks about abstract ideas and distorted or only partially correct ideas of things, he obviously could not hold such a naive theory. He uses words like "reflect" and "copy" to indicate that our ideas are true to the extent that they correspond with reality.

The political point of difference between Marx and Lenin is supposed to be that Lenin believed in a strong socialist state — a "dictatorship of the proletariat" — which would defend the working class against its enemies and administer the building of socialism. Marx is said to shun such a concept. The *phrase* "dictatorship of the

163

proletariat" is associated in bourgeois propaganda with Stalinism and other real or supposed anti-democratic tendencies in socialism. This is, of course, not what Lenin had in mind. (In fact, in the last year of his life he warned against Stalin and his high-handed methods.) However the *concept* of a worker's state is central to any theory that is sincere about wanting not only to win socialism but also to build and defend it. Marx saw this just as clearly as Lenin.

The concept is present in the *Communist Manifesto*. In a well-known letter written in 1852 (to J. Weydemeyer, March 5) Marx wrote:

> . . . what I did that was new was to prove: (1) that the *existence of classes* is only bound up with *particular historical phases in the development of production,* (2) that the class struggle necessarily leads to the *dictatorship of the proletariat,* (3) that this dictatorship itself only constitutes the transition of the *abolition of all classes* and to a *classless society.*

In a critique of some reformist socialists written in 1875 ("Critique of the Gotha Programme") Marx again maintained:

> Between capitalist and communist society lies the period of the revolutionary transformation of the one into the other. Corresponding to this is also a political transition period in which the state can be nothing but the *revolutionary dictatorship of the proletariat.*

The truth of the matter is that on the most basic philosophical and political points Marx, Engels and Lenin agreed. They agreed because all three were dedicated, practical scientific humanists and revolutionaries.

READINGS FOR APPENDIX

K. Marx, *The Economic and Philosophic Manuscripts of 1844* (New York, New World Paperbacks 1967, reprinted 1976). This complete edition of Marx's "Paris Manuscripts" includes a useful introduction and notes by the Marxist scholar, Dirk Struik.

K. Marx, *Writings of the Young Marx on Philosophy and Society,* edited by L. Easton and K. Guddat (New York, Doubleday, 1967). In addition to the 1844 Manuscripts, this includes many other early essays and articles by Marx.

Franz Mehring, *Karl Marx: The Story of His Life* (London, 1936 and Ann Arbor, paperback, 1962). This very thorough biography of Marx and Engels was written by a contemporary of theirs.

John Hoffman, *Marxism and the Theory of Praxis* (New York, International Publishers, 1976). A good criticism of those who have attempted to de-Marxize Marxism in its own name.

The passage from Marx's high school essay is quoted in Franz Mehring, *Karl Marx, the Story of His Life* (London, 1936 and Ann Arbor, 1962), p. 5. The passage from *Capital* is in the Preface to the first edition, and the one from the *German Ideology* is on p. 49 of the 1976 Moscow edition. Both the letter to Weydemeyer and the "Critique of the Gotha Programme" can be found in *Karl Marx & Frederick Engels, Selected Works* (New York, New World Paperbacks, 1969). The comment by Marx on Ricardo is in K. Marx, *On Malthus* (New York, 1954), p. 120. The letter to Weydemeyer can also be found on p. 64 of *Marx and Engels, Selected Correspondence* (Moscow, 1975), along with other letters and important correspondence between Marx and Engels.

INDEX OF DEFINITIONS

This index lists pages on which some key terms used by Marxists are defined. The index is intended only as an aid to the reader and not to indicate formal and detailed definitions, since these would be inappropriate in an introductory book. For more detailed definitions texts referred to in chapter readings should be consulted. While there is basic agreement among Marxists on the meanings of most of these terms, there are also differences of opinion about the exact definitions of some terms. This is in keeping with the Marxist view that since there are no hard and fast boundaries separating things, and since everything changes, therefore scientists in all fields, including scientific socialists, must constantly review, sharpen and improve their definitions.